All the Places to Go . . .
How Will You Know?

Tyndale House Publishers, Inc.
Carol Stream, Illinois

JOHN ORTBERG

ALL THE
PLACES
TO GO

HOW WILL YOU KNOW?

God has placed before you
an open door.
What will you do?

Visit Tyndale online at www.tyndale.com.

TYNDALE and Tyndale's quill logo are registered trademarks of Tyndale House Publishers, Inc.

Designed by Jacqueline L. Nuñez

Edited by Jonathan Schindler

Published in association with Yates & Yates (www.yates2.com).

Library of Congress Cataloging-in-Publication Data

Ortberg, John.

    All the places to go . . . how will you know? : God has placed before you an open door. What will you do? / John Ortberg.

      pages cm

    Includes bibliographical references.

    ISBN 978-1-4143-7900-5 (hc)

1. Christian life. I. Title.

    BV4501.3.O763 2015

248.4—dc23   2014036431

ISBN 978-1-4143-7901-2 Softcover
ISBN 978-1-4964-0611-8 ITPE edition

Printed in the United States of America

22   21   20   19   18   17
10   9   8   7   6   5

To Barbara Lynn (Ortberg) Harrison and Barton David Ortberg, with whom I snuck through the secret gates and open doors of childhood, and who courageously walk through them still, this book is most gratefully dedicated.

Contents

CHAPTER I

ALL THE PLACES TO GO . . . HOW WILL YOU KNOW?

IF YOU HAD TO SUMMARIZE your life in six words, what would they be?

Several years ago an online magazine asked that question. It was inspired by a possibly legendary challenge posed to Ernest Hemingway to write a six-word story that resulted in the classic "For sale: baby shoes, never worn."

The magazine was flooded with so many responses that the site almost crashed, and the responses were eventually turned into a book. *Not Quite What I Was Planning* is filled with six-word memoirs by writers "famous and obscure." The memoirs range from funny to ironic to inspiring to heartbreaking:

- "One tooth, one cavity; life's cruel."
- "Savior complex makes for many disappointments."
- "Cursed with cancer. Blessed with friends." (This one was written not by a wise, old grandmother but by a nine-year-old boy with thyroid cancer.)
- "The psychic said I'd be richer." (Actually, this author might be richer if she stopped blowing money on psychics.)
- "Tombstone won't say: 'Had health insurance.'"
- "Not a good Christian, but trying."
- "Thought I would have more impact."[1]

The challenge of the six-word limitation is its demand to focus on what matters most, to capture briefly something of significance. Winston Churchill once sent a dessert pudding back to the kitchen because "it lacked a theme." I don't want my life to be like Winston's pudding.

It is striking to think about what the characters of Scripture might write for their six-word memoirs. I think they would revolve around the intersection of the story of that person's life with God's story. They would all be inspired by a divine opportunity that God had set before them and the response—the yes or no—that shaped their lives.

- Abraham: "Left Ur. Had baby. Still laughing."
- Jonah: "'No.' Storm. Overboard. Whale. Regurgitated. 'Yes.'"
- Moses: "Burning bush. Stone tablets. Charlton Heston."
- Adam: "Eyes opened, but can't find home."
- Shadrach, Meshach, and Abednego: "King was hot. Furnace was not."
- Noah: "Hated the rain, loved the rainbow."
- Esau: "At least the stew was good."
- Esther: "Eye candy. Mordecai handy. Israel dandy."
- Mary: "Manger. Pain. Joy. Cross. Pain. Joy."
- Prodigal Son: "Bad. Sad. Dad glad. Brother mad."
- Rich Young Ruler: "Jesus called. Left sad. Still rich."
- Zacchaeus: "Climbed sycamore tree. Short, poorer, happier."
- Woman caught in adultery: "Picked up man, put down stones."
- Good Samaritan: "I came, I saw, I stopped."
- Paul: "Damascus. Blind. Suffer. Write. Change world."

"Not quite what I was planning" is the six-word memoir any of them could have written. In none of these cases would these characters have been able to predict where their lives would take them. They were interrupted. They were offered an opportunity or threatened by danger or both. This is how life works. We are neither the authors nor the pawns of our life stories but rather partners somehow with fate or destiny or circumstance or providence. And the writers of Scripture insist that, at least sometimes, in at least some lives—in any lives where the person is willing—that unseen Partner can be God.

Often in the Bible these opportunities seem to come in unmistakable packages. A burning bush. A wrestling angel. Handwriting on the wall. A fleece. A voice. A dream. A talking donkey like in *Shrek*.

But there is another picture of God-inspired opportunity sprinkled across Scripture that is easier for me to relate to. It is a picture of divine possibility that still comes to every life. It is a picture I have loved since my college professor Jerry Hawthorne introduced it to me:

> To the angel of the church in Philadelphia write:
> "These are the words of him who is holy and true,
> who holds the key of David. What he opens no
> one can shut, and what he shuts no one can open.
> I know your deeds. See, I have placed before you *an
> open door* that no one can shut. I know that you have
> little strength, yet you have kept my word and have
> not denied my name." (Revelation 3:7-8, emphasis
> mine)

A door, Dr. Hawthorne said, is one of the richest images in literature. It can mean safety ("my door is chained and locked") or hiddenness ("no one knows what goes on behind closed doors"). It can mean rejection ("she shut the door in my face") or rest (young mothers' favorite room is the bathroom, where they can close the door and be alone).

But in this passage a door means none of those things. Rather, it is an *open* door, symbolic of "boundless opportunities. Of unlimited chances to do something worthwhile; of grand openings into new and unknown adventures of significant living; of heretofore unimagined chances to do good, to make our lives count for eternity."[2]

An open door is the great adventure of life because it means the possibility of being useful to God. The offer of it, and our response to it, is the subject of this book.

God Can Open a Door for Anybody

When my dad was soon to turn fifty, my mom asked him abruptly in the kitchen one day, "John, is this all we're going to do for the rest of our lives? Just this same routine of going to work and talking to the same people?" My dad, a very stable CPA who had lived in Rockford, Illinois, his whole life and never thought of living anywhere else, said, "I guess." But he started wondering if there might be something more.

Often an open door to another room begins with a sense of discontent about the room you're already in.

Very unexpectedly, through my wife, my dad was offered a job by a church in Southern California. However, it would have been a pretty radical move—two thousand miles away from the only place he'd ever lived, in a job he wasn't trained for, with people he didn't know. After checking it out, he told the church leaders that it just wouldn't work: the salary was too low, the houses were too expensive, the career shift was too big, the pension was too small, he was too old, and the people were too weird.

It was the right decision, he thought. It would have been too big a risk. He breathed a sigh of relief and went home.

But strange things began to happen after he said no. My dad had a dream one night where it seemed God was saying to him, "John, if you stay on this course, you will neither sow nor reap." My dad was from a very nonemotional, non-demonstrative Swedish church where people might talk to God but never expect God to talk to them. They didn't even talk to each other much. So he didn't make much of the dream.

When he woke up, he read in my mom's journal—something else he'd never done—where she had written, "I don't know how to pray for John; I don't think he's doing what God wants him to do."

All this made him not want to go to church, so he stayed home but ended up seeing a TV church service where the preacher said, "If proof is possible, faith is impossible." It struck him that he had wanted proof that if he took this new job, everything would work out okay. But if the preacher was right, such proof would rule out the very thing God wanted most, which was my dad's faith.

So the next week he went back to church. The sermon was on the ABCs of faith: that you must *abandon* your old life, *believe* God's promises are trustworthy, and *commit* to a new journey.

So my dad got on a plane to go back to California, even though the pastor of the California church said they were now looking at other candidates. While on the plane, he opened his Bible and happened to read a passage where God promised people that if they abandoned their idols of gold and silver, the time would come when they would reap and sow.

He more or less took all of this as an open door.

Recently my sister, my brother, and I spent three days together with my parents to celebrate my dad's eightieth birthday. He's retired now, as is my mom, but they moved to that church in California, and both were on staff there for a quarter of a century, and it was the great, risky, thrilling adventure of their lives.

We wrote out eighty cards, eighty memories of life with my dad. It was amazing how many memories came flooding back—my dad's voice when he'd read to us when we were young; the math flash cards he'd use to teach us; the scent of his Aramis cologne I would borrow for dates.

But the most dramatic card in my dad's jar, the decision that divided his life into Before and After, was his choice to go through an open door that he did not initiate, never expected, and felt unprepared for.

"I know that your strength is small," God says to the church at Philadelphia. People in the church may not have been hugely flattered when they read that line. But what a gift to know that open doors are not reserved for the specially talented or the extraordinarily strong. God can open a door for anyone.

God Can Open a Door in Any Circumstance

Viktor Frankl was a brilliant doctor whom the Nazis imprisoned in a concentration camp. They took away his livelihood, confiscated his possessions, mocked his dignity, and killed his family. They locked him in a cell with no way out. A room without an open door is a prison. But he found a door that his guards did not know about: "Everything can be taken from a man but one thing: the last of the human freedoms—to choose one's attitude in any given set of circumstances, to choose one's own way."[3]

Frankl discovered that doors are not just physical. A door is a choice. He found that when his circumstances had closed every outer door to him, they revealed to him the doors that matter far more—the doors through which a soul can leave fear and enter into courage, leave hatred and enter into forgiveness, leave ignorance and enter into learning. He discovered that his guards were actually far more imprisoned—by cruelty and ignorance and foolish obedience to barbarism—than he was imprisoned by walls and barbed wire.

Some people learn this and become free; some never see it and live as prisoners. There is always a door.

Columbia researcher Sheena Iyengar has found that the average person makes about seventy conscious decisions every day.[4] That's 25,550 decisions a year. Over seventy years, that's 1,788,500 decisions. Albert Camus said, "Life is a sum of all your choices." You put all those 1,788,500 choices together, and that's who you are.

The ability to recognize doors—to discover the range of

possibilities that lie before us in every moment and in any circumstance—is a skill that can be learned. It brings the possibility of God's presence and power into any situation on earth. People who study entrepreneurs say they excel in something called "opportunity alertness." They look at the same circumstances as everyone else, but they "notice without search opportunities that have hitherto been overlooked." They are "alert, waiting, continually receptive to something that may turn up."[5] Perhaps there is a kind of "divine opportunity alertness" we can cultivate.

Sometimes the opportunity doesn't involve going to a new place; it means finding a new and previously unrecognized opportunity in the old place. In a sense, this is the surprising story of the nation of Israel. Israel thought it was on a journey to national greatness, with a powerful army and abundant wealth. Instead, it knew exile and oppression. But with the closed door of national greatness came an open door to a kind of spiritual greatness. Israel changed the spiritual and moral life of the world. And while nations like Assyria and Babylon and Persia have come and gone, Israel's gift to humanity remains.

Open doors in the Bible never exist just for the sake of the people offered them. They involve opportunity, but it's the opportunity to bless someone else. An open door may be thrilling to me, but it doesn't exist solely for my benefit.

An open door is not just a picture of something good. It involves a good that we do not yet fully know. An open door does not offer a complete view of the future. An open door means opportunity, mystery, possibility—but not a guarantee.

God doesn't say, "I've set before you a hammock."

He doesn't say, "I've set before you a detailed set of instructions about exactly what you should do and exactly what will happen as a result."

An open door doesn't mean all will be pleasant and smooth on the other side. One of those six-word memoirs looks like Jesus could have written it: "Savior complex makes for many disappointments." An open door is not a blueprint or a guarantee.

It's an open door. To find out what's on the other side, you'll have to go through.

God Can Open Doors Very Quietly

God often does not tell us which door to choose. This is one of God's most frustrating characteristics.

Many years ago my wife, Nancy, and I stood before an open door. We faced a choice to move across the country—from California, which was Nancy's lifelong home, to a church called Willow Creek near Chicago. It was a very difficult decision between going to that church in Chicago and staying in California. We were driving on the decision-making journey the same day, on the same freeway, that O. J. Simpson made his famous low-speed escape run in his white Bronco.

I leaned toward Chicago because I thought if I didn't go there, I'd always wonder what might have been. (We're marked by the doors we go through and by the ones we don't.) Nancy leaned toward California because the church in Chicago was in Chicago. We thought and prayed and talked and talked some more. Choosing a door is rarely easy. I was haunted by the fear of getting it wrong. What if God wanted me to choose door #1 but I chose door #2? Why couldn't he have made the choice plainer?

We do not always get to know which door we're supposed to go through. Jesus says to the church in Philadelphia, "I have placed before you an open door" (Revelation 3:8). But he does not specify which door it is. I can only imagine their questions. *How will we know? Are we supposed to vote on it? What if we go through the wrong one?*

This has been an ironic and often painful part of my life. God opens doors but then doesn't seem to tell me which ones I'm supposed to go through.

I come from a long line of preachers, with a long line of stories about how they got their "call." My great-grandfather, Robert Bennett Hall, ran away from an orphanage when he was twelve and ended up working for a shopkeeper and marrying his daughter. One day he was sweeping out the store when he got the call, put down his broom, went home, and told my great-grandmother that he'd been called to be a preacher.

My brother-in-law, Craig, was working at a grocery store when he received what was to him an unmistakable summons to become a pastor. He got his call in the frozen foods section.

I never got a call—at least not one like that. I used to hang out in grocery stores sometimes, but I never got a call. It took me many years to understand that God may have very good reasons to leave choices up to us rather than sending us e-mails telling us what to do.

When the invitation to go to Chicago came, I faced the same dilemma. If pastors change churches, they're supposed to have a clear call—especially if the new church is bigger than the old one. Pastors will usually say things like "I didn't want to go anywhere, but I got this strange sense of unrest in my spirit, and I had to obey." Pastors almost never say stuff like "This new church is way bigger than my old church, and I am super excited about that."

But I had thoughts like that. I knew they weren't my best thoughts, or my only thoughts, but they were in the mix. And I had to struggle with them. I think maybe that's part of why God works through open doors. They help us struggle with our real dreams and motives.

So Nancy and I wrestled with this decision. As we were considering what to do, my friend Jon gave me a book that had recently been written and which I had never read. It was by a man named Dr. Seuss, whom I had never consulted for career guidance. He had written:

> *You have brains in your head.*
> *You have feet in your shoes.*
> *You can steer yourself any direction you choose. . . .*
>
> *Oh, the places you'll go! . . .*
>
> *Except when you don't.*
> *Because, sometimes, you won't.*[6]

Oh, the places you'll go. This was the promise that came to all those characters in the Bible. This is the promise of the God of the open door.

I think Dr. Seuss's words resonate so deeply with thousands of graduates every year because what matters is not a guarantee about the outcome. What matters is the adventure of the journey. That's what struck me when I first read the book.

I thought about my parents and the great adventure of their lives in moving from Illinois to California. I thought about how sharp my dad's regret was when he said the safe no and how keen his joy was when he said a risky yes.

We ultimately decided to go to Chicago. We got no divine direction or supernatural indicators as far as we could tell. But we chose it because the adventure of yes seemed more alive than the safety of no.

Very rarely in the Bible does God come to someone and say, "Stay." Almost never does God interrupt someone and ask them to remain in comfort, safety, and familiarity. He opens a door and calls them to come through it.

The staggering truth is that this very moment is alive with opportunity. What could you be doing right this moment that you aren't? You could be learning to speak Chinese. You could be training for a marathon. You could be logging on to eHarmony to search for—and possibly meet—the love of your life. You could be telling a friend a secret you've never told another living soul. You could be sponsoring an impoverished child. You could be watching *The Bachelor*, or buying the world's sharpest knife from an infomercial, or finally making that therapy appointment your spouse has been encouraging you to make for years.

There's an open door.

But wait! There's more. "Open door" isn't a phrase to describe just any opportunity. An open door is an opportunity provided by God, to act *with* God and *for* God. In that little passage to the church at Philadelphia, the apostle John has a wonderful expression. He writes that what stands before the church is literally an *opened* door. Jewish writers often avoided writing the word *God* directly, out of reverence. So this is John's way of saying that the opportunity being offered did not come out of the blue. God was at work. What lies before us is more than merely human. Not simply open doors, but *opened* doors.

The beginning of the story of God's people comes with the unexpected offer of an opened door. It came to a man named Abram, under the category of not-quite-what-I-was-planning. God began it all by approaching an elderly couple before Israel even existed:

Abram and Sarai, today is the day!
So get your dad, Terah, and get on your way.

You will wander like nomads, and I even think maybe
You might have a nonagenarian baby.

You'll be marked by your faith, you'll be marked by a
*   vision,*
You'll be marked by (you might not love this) circumcision.

Like stars in the sky your descendants will be,
Though you will tell lies indiscriminately.

You'll get lost and confused and be badly afraid.
You will wait till quite late and mistakes will be made.

You won't know what to say, you won't know what to do,
But all peoples on earth will get blessings through you.

With your muddled-up faith you'll do more than you know,
And I promise you this: Oh, the places you'll go!

And they went. In a sense, the whole story of the Bible hinges on this moment. The writer of Genesis expresses it in two words: *Wayyelech Avram.* "Abram went."

Not quite what I was planning.

Oh, the places you'll *wayyelech.*

God Can Use a "Wrong Door" to Shape a Right Heart

In the New Testament, James says that if any of us lacks wisdom, we should ask God for some. He doesn't say we should ask which door to go through but for the tools to choose wisely.

God's primary will for your life is not the achievements you accrue; it's the person you become. God's primary will for your life is not what job you ought to take; it's not primarily situational or circumstantial. It's not mainly the city where you live or whether you get married or what house you ought to be in. God's primary will for your life is that you become a magnificent person in his image, somebody with the character of Jesus. That is God's main will for your life. No circumstance can prevent that.

We all understand that, especially parents. If you're a parent, would you want the kind of kids you have to tell their whole lives, "Wear these clothes. Take these classes. Go to that school. Apply for this job. Marry that person. Purchase this house," and you always have them do exactly what you tell them as long as they live? ("No" is the correct answer here. No, you wouldn't want that.)

Why? Because your main goal is not for them to be little robots that carry out instructions; your goal is that they become people of great character and judgment. The only way for them to do that is to make lots and lots of decisions. Of course, that means they'll make a lot of the wrong decisions. That becomes a primary way they learn.

Very often God's will for you will be "I want you to decide," because decision making is an indispensable part of character formation. God is primarily in the character-forming business, not the circumstance-shaping business.

And God is in the open-door business. This means a new way of looking at God. He prefers yes to no. He loves adventure and opportunity.

This means a new way of looking at life. I do not have to be afraid of failure. I do not have to live in fear over circumstance. Each moment is an opportunity to look for a door that opens up into God and his presence.

This means a new way of looking at myself. I am no longer limited by my smallness and weakness. The God who opens the door to me is also the God who knows how small and weak I am.

This means a new way of choosing. I no longer have to live under the tyranny of the perfect choice. God can use even what looks like the "wrong door" if I go through it with the right heart.

Our lives are filled with doors.

Perhaps you are facing graduation. According to one recent survey, more than anything else, young adults want to work at a job that inspires them and that offers autonomy.[7] You want to follow your bliss, but maybe your bliss hasn't shown up yet.

Maybe you are in transition. People are changing jobs, companies, and whole careers more often than ever before. How do you choose wisely?

Maybe you are in a rut. Your life is safe but not fulfilling. You have a desire to do more or be more.

Maybe you're facing an empty nest. You suddenly have freedom and time and possibilities that haven't been available in a few decades. What is the best way to spend them?

Maybe you're retiring. But you know the word *retire* isn't in the Bible, and you're not ready for death or shuffleboard. What might God have next for you?

Maybe you're facing rapid change. Career specialist Andy Chan notes that young adults will face, on average, twenty-nine jobs over the course of their lives. Oxford researchers predict that over the next two decades about half the jobs that exist today will be replaced by technology.[8] How do you adapt to a changing environment?

Maybe you have a passion. You have traveled overseas and seen a great need, or you have studied a problem and want to make a difference. What's your next step?

Perhaps you're a student trying to decide what school to attend or what major to choose. What if you choose a major that isn't in line with your ultimate career? (By the way, everyone chooses a major that isn't in line with their career. Tell your parents not to worry.)

Perhaps you're on the brink of an exciting relationship or thinking about marriage. How do you know if this person is "the one"? What if you choose wrong?

Or perhaps you have been frustrated by a lost opportunity in your past. Does God still have another for you?

Many people get confused about decision making and "God's will for my life." As we will see, learning to recognize and go through open doors is a learned skill. Most often we learn best by starting with small doors—a word of kindness or an act of service or a risk of confrontation or a prayer of trust.

Every morning is an open door; every moment can become one. Some of us see the doors and seize them, and so life becomes a divine adventure. Some of us shrink back or fail to see. A room with no door is a prison. To fail to embrace the open door is to miss the work God has made for us to do. If we want to experience more of the Spirit of God in our lives, we need to train ourselves to look for and respond to moments of divine opportunity.

Every door you take means leaving something and arriving somewhere. How will it change your life? What will it cost?

Every journey—yours, too—will be filled with uncertainty and mystery and adventure and frustration and surprise.

From the beginning, God's open doors meet people's closed hearts. Abram said,

Where are these places you want me to go?
When will I get there? How will I know?

Will I need a design? Will I need a degree?
Will I need other things that you're hiding from me?

Where is the map of your plan for my life?
I must know all this stuff. I must talk to my wife.

I'm old. I'm not bold. And you're leaving things out.
There are bales of details you must tell me about!

And lo! The Lord didn't tell him. The Lord is notoriously fuzzy about details like that. Knowing too many details would take all the excitement out of the adventure. God wanted Abram to be his friend, and friends trust each other, and you can't learn to trust someone without a little risk and uncertainty and vulnerability.

God told Abram, "Go to the place I will show you."

Oh, the places you'll go!

That's where the open door leads. To the place where God guides.

God opened a door. Abram went. And the rest is history. Where will your doors lead?

CHAPTER 2

OPEN-DOOR PEOPLE AND CLOSED-DOOR PEOPLE

THE COLLEGE I ATTENDED had compulsory chapel services. Monitors—affectionately known as "chapel spies"—sat in special seats to take attendance, so each semester the college had to find some systematic way to assign chapel seats. Usually we were arranged by alphabetical order or major or home state. One semester the chapel spies sat us by SAT scores. Word of this leaked out about three weeks into the semester. We realized people could figure out how smart we were by where we were sitting—higher SAT scores were toward the front, and lower SAT scores were toward the back. News of this triggered a small-scale riot. The chapel powers had to reseat the whole student body and throw out attendance records for the first month.

Who cares if other people know how smart we are, right?

Well, researcher Carol Dweck says it turns out there are two kinds of people in the world: one of them cares a great deal, and the other doesn't care much at all. And this, in turn, is connected to whether we are the kind of people likely to go through open doors.

Dweck explores mind-sets and people's ability to navigate adversity. She is particularly interested in how people handle limitations, obstacles, failure, and change. In one study, she took a group of ten-year-olds and gave them increasingly difficult math problems to see how they would handle failure. Most students got discouraged and depressed, but a few had a totally different response. One kid—in the face of failure—rubbed his hands together, smacked his lips, and said, "I love a challenge!" Another kid, failing one math problem after another, said, "You know, I was hoping this would be informative."

"What's wrong with them?" Dweck wondered. "I always thought you coped with failure or you didn't cope with failure. I never thought anyone *loved* failure. Were these alien children or were they on to something?"[1]

Dweck realized that not only were these kids not discouraged by failure, they didn't think they were failing. They thought they were *learning*. She came to the conclusion that human beings have two different, almost opposite mind-sets about life. One of them I'm going to call a "closed mind-set." Those with a closed mind-set believe that life is full of a fixed amount of gifts and talents, and their worth depends on how talented they are. Therefore, their job is to convince others that they've got "it," whatever "it" is.

If that's the way I think about my life, then of course going through open doors is mostly something to be avoided, because every time there is a challenge, my worth is on the line. I might not have enough "it." I'll try to arrange my life so I always have success and never fail. I never, ever want to make a mistake, because if I make a mistake, people might think I don't have "it."

We see this early on. Kids in school, if there's a big test, will sometimes say to other kids, "You know, I didn't even study for this test." Why would they say that? Because that way if they get a bad grade on the test and others find out, the other kids won't think they're not smart. They're still smart. They still have "it." Then if they get a good grade and other kids think they didn't study, they have even more of "it."

This is why everybody at my college got all shook up about being seated by SAT scores—except the people in the front row. (By the way, I was seated in the balcony. But it's because I hadn't gotten much sleep the night before the test. Plus, I didn't really try my hardest. Actually, I took the ACT. Not that I care what you think anyway.)

Dweck said there's another way to go through life, and

that's with what might be called an "open mind-set." Those with an open mind-set believe that what matters is not raw ability; what matters is growth. Growth is always possible. A commitment to growth means they embrace challenge, so the goal is not trying to look smarter or more competent than other people. The goal is to grow beyond where they are today. Therefore, failure is indispensable and something to be learned from.

Ultimately, faith provides the greatest foundation for an open mind-set. The reason I don't have to prove my worth is that I am loved by God no matter what. The reason I can be open to tomorrow is that God is already there.

We must abandon a closed-door way of looking at God, our lives, and ourselves if we are to respond to the open door. Closed-door thinking may disguise itself as prudence or common sense, but it's really a refusal to trust God because of fear. Closed-door thinking is David's brothers saying that Goliath can't be fought. It's the Israelites telling Joshua and Caleb that their enemies are like giants and the Israelites are like grasshoppers, so they should return to Egypt and slavery. It's the Rich Young Ruler deciding that discipleship would be nice, but it's a little overpriced. It's me every time I choose hoarding over generosity or silence over speaking hard truth in love. It's me when I claim to believe in God, but when he says, "Go," I stay. I'm a Staytheist. Closed-door thinking looks safe, but it's the most dangerous thinking of all because it leaves God on the other side of the door.

To be an open-door person means to embrace an open

mind-set—along with a set of disciplines and practices to help us regularly embrace and walk through open doors. Let's look at some characteristics of open-door people that make them more likely to walk through God's open doors.

Open-Door People Are Ready, "Ready or Not"

Open doors always seem scarier than closed ones. We never know for sure what will happen when we go through.

When we have big choices to make—taking a job, making a move, getting into a relationship, having a baby—we all want to know ahead of time, "What exactly are we getting into?"

We never know.

And that's a very good thing, because a lot of times if we knew what we were getting into, we wouldn't get into it in the first place. Frederick Buechner says, "God's coming is always unforeseen, I think, and the reason, if I had to guess, is that if he gave us anything much in the way of advance warning, more often than not we would have made ourselves scarce long before he got there."[2]

The truth about being ready is you'll never be ready. When our first child was born, Nancy had gotten a kidney infection, so on top of having just given birth, she was sick. At one point she started to freak out: "What if the baby gets sick? What if one of us drops her? What if we discipline her too much? What if we discipline her too little? What if we are too unhealthy? What if we mess her up for her whole life?"

I explained patiently, "Nancy, we can always have more children."

Just about every parent I've ever known, when they get that first kid home, finds him- or herself thinking, *I don't think I'm ready for this.* Then that kid grows up, and it's time for the kid to leave home and face the world, but the world is scary and expensive, and the kid says, "I don't think I'm ready for this." And the parents say, "Ready or not . . . "

There's a whole syndrome around this fear called "failure to launch." People are often afraid to go through economic independence, vocational direction, and relational open doors because they don't feel ready. But the world says, "Ready or not, here I come."

Life, opportunities, challenges, relationships, eventually aging, ultimately dying—all these have a way of saying, "Ready or not, here I come."

Life's inevitability doesn't mean that preparation is unimportant. I'd rather have a brain surgeon who has taken a few classes ahead of time than a complete newbie. But "feeling ready" is not the ultimate criterion for determining the places you'll go.

God says, "I have set before you an open door," not "I have set before you a finished script." An open door is a beginning, an opportunity, but it has no guaranteed ending. It's not a sneak peek at the finish. If it is to be entered, it can be entered only by faith.

"Feeling ready" is highly overrated. God is looking for obedience. When God brought the people of Israel into the Promised Land, he had them step into the Jordan first, *then* he parted the river. If they had waited for proof, they'd be standing on the banks still. Faith grows when God says to somebody, "Go," and that person says yes.

Maybe the greatest open door in the Bible comes at the end of the Gospel of Matthew. Jesus sends his disciples out to change the world, but there are two striking problems. One is that there are only eleven disciples. All through the Gospel the number twelve reminds readers that the disciples have been chosen to be a picture of the redeemed, restarted twelve tribes of Israel. Twelve is the number of wholeness, completeness, readiness. Now they don't have enough players.

But it's not just that they have the wrong number. "When they saw him, they worshiped him; but some doubted" (Matthew 28:17). They had a *quantity* problem; now they have a *quality* problem. They don't have enough disciples, and the ones they do have don't believe enough.

New Testament scholar Dale Bruner writes, "The number 'eleven' limps; it is not perfect like twelve. . . . The church that Jesus sends into the world is 'elevenish,' imperfect, fallible."[3]

This is the group Jesus chooses to change the world. He doesn't say, "First, let's get enough numbers" or "First, let's get enough faith." He just says, "You go. We'll work on the faith thing and the numbers thing while you're doing the obedience thing. I'm sending you out. Ready or not . . . "

In the Bible, when God calls someone to do something, no one responds by saying, "I'm ready":

- Moses: "I have never been eloquent. . . . I am slow of speech and tongue" (Exodus 4:10).

- Gideon: "How can I save Israel? My clan is the weakest in Manasseh, and I am the least in my family" (Judges 6:15).
- Abraham: "Will a son be born to a man a hundred years old?" (Genesis 17:17).
- Jeremiah: "Alas, Sovereign LORD, . . . I am too young" (Jeremiah 1:6).
- Isaiah: "Woe to me . . . for I am a man of unclean lips" (Isaiah 6:5).
- Esther: "For any man or woman who approaches the king . . . without being summoned the king has but one law: that they be put to death" (Esther 4:11).
- Rich Young Ruler: "He went away sad, because he had great wealth" (Matthew 19:22).
- Ruth: "There was a famine in the land" (Ruth 1:1).
- Saul: (Samuel was going to anoint Saul king; the people couldn't find him and asked if he was present.) "The LORD said, 'See, he has hidden himself among the baggage'" (1 Samuel 10:22, NRSV).

Too inarticulate, too weak, too old, too young, too sinful, too dangerous, too rich, too poor, too much baggage—no one *ever* says, "Okay, Lord—I feel *ready*." And God says to us what he has always said, what Jesus said to his disciples: "Ready or not . . . "

The truth is you don't know what you can do until you actually do it. "Ready" comes faster if you're already moving. If you wait to move until you're fully ready, you'll wait until you die. Jesus doesn't say, "Go; you're ready." He says, "Go; I'll go with you."

Years ago a friend took me up a mountain for a surprise. He had signed me up to go hang gliding in the San Gabriel Mountains. I was told you just stand on a ledge, look off a cliff, and then jump. If the chute didn't hold air—well, my wife would be dating again soon.

So there I was, standing on the edge of a cliff, looking down. The instructors asked me, "Are you ready?"

I knew I wasn't ready. But I was connected to someone. The instructors have you go in tandem, and the person I was connected to was ready. The instructors yelled, "Ready or not!" And when my partner went, I went.

What I didn't know until we landed was that it was my partner's first time too. My partner didn't know enough even to be afraid. And I thought, *That's the last time I go hang gliding with a ten-year-old girl.*

Jesus takes his friends up a mountain. Not enough of them. Not enough faith. Doesn't matter. What matters isn't whether they're ready. What matters is that *he's* ready. And you and I never know when he's ready. He's in charge of that.

Open-Door People Are Unhindered by Uncertainty

One of the big problems with open doors is that they're not always well marked. When God does call, the call may not always be clear. As a general rule, with God, information is given on a need-to-know basis, and God decides who needs to know what, when.

A classic example of this comes in the book of Acts. The church has to decide if God is calling them to include Gentiles in a radical new way. After much prayer they send out a letter: "It seemed good to the Holy Spirit and to us . . . " (Acts 15:28).

Really? "It *seemed* good"? The future of the entire human race is at stake, and the best you can do is "it *seemed . . .* "?

And yet the church leaders were quite comfortable sending out this letter. God could have put an ad on Craigslist: "Now accepting Gentile applicants." But apparently his will for his people was that they should not be told exactly what his will was. Apparently, he knew they would grow more if they had to think and debate and argue it out than if they got a memo. And apparently, they didn't demand certainty. They were willing to settle for sincere obedience.

From the beginning of God's interactions with humanity, he seems to give information on a need-to-know basis. Ambiguity and uncertainty are woven into the story from the beginning.

The first eleven chapters of Genesis involve big themes: Creation, Fall, Judgment—but all that is leading to a moment in Genesis 12 when things narrow down to the smallest scale. God is going to come now to one ordinary individual. Not a king on a giant stage—just one regular person. It could be you. It could be me. We never know ahead of time the full significance of the doors we face.

We are told that a man named Terah lived in a city called Ur of the Chaldeans. He had been born there. One day he moved. He took his family—which included his childless son Abram and Abram's wife, Sarai—and "together they set out from Ur of the Chaldeans to go to Canaan. But when they came to Harran, they settled there. Terah lived 205 years, and he died in Harran" (Genesis 11:31-32).

The story goes on:

> The LORD had said to Abram, "Go from your country, your people and your father's household to the land I will show you. I will make you into a great nation, and I will bless you; I will make your name great, and you will be a blessing. I will bless those who bless you, and whoever curses you I will curse; and all peoples on earth will be blessed through you."
>
> So Abram went, as the LORD had told him; and Lot went with him. Abram was seventy-five years old when he set out from Harran. He took his wife Sarai, his nephew Lot, all the possessions they had accumulated and the people they had acquired in Harran, and they set out for the land of Canaan, and they arrived there. (Genesis 12:1-5)

In the account, God says, "Go," and there are two parts to God's "go." There are always two parts to God's "go": going from and going to. God says, "Go from your country—the land that's familiar to you—and from your people, from the culture that has shaped you, and from your father's household. Leave home."

The first readers of this story would have understood that when God came to Abram's family, Ur was perhaps the largest city in the world. About 2,000 BC it was *the* great place. All the trading wealth from around the Mediterranean that was headed into ancient Mesopotamia had to pass through Ur. It was a place of great wealth, of great trade, of great learning, of great technology. The first written legal code that began civilization was there in Ur. Ur was a difficult place to leave.

God said to Abram, "Leave Ur. Go to the land I will show you." That's . . . kind of vague.

Open-door people are comfortable with ambiguity and risk. Or, if not comfortable with it, at least they decide not to allow it to paralyze them.

"The land I will show you" turned out to be Canaan. Now Canaan was everything Ur was not. It was uncultured, uncivilized, undeveloped, uncultivated—a rough, difficult place. Nobody who could afford to live in Ur, the great capital of civilization, would set out for Canaan. It would be a little like someone moving from Manhattan to Minot, North Dakota. (I have friends from there who tell me the town's slogan is "Why not Minot?")

Nobody who was looking for opportunity would leave Ur of the Chaldeans to go to Canaan. But God's open doors are not always obvious. They are not primarily designed to open to wealth or status. Going through open doors means I will have to be able to trust God with my future when the path I'm called to take does not look like the obvious one.

The big question for Abram is, "Why? Why do you want

me to leave?" The text doesn't say, but we actually have a good idea, and this will relate to you and me. Later in the Bible, God says to Israel, "Long ago your ancestors, including Terah the father of Abraham and Nahor, lived beyond the Euphrates River and worshiped other gods. But I took your father Abraham from the land beyond the Euphrates and led him throughout Canaan and gave him many descendants" (Joshua 24:2-3).

Abram had received a cultural inheritance of idolatry. The problem with idols from a biblical perspective is not simply that they get God's *name* wrong, it's that they get God's *character* wrong. Idols, from a biblical perspective, offer power but do not demand what the Lord requires: "to act justly and to love mercy and to walk humbly with your God" (Micah 6:8). Idolatry involves a system of beliefs and attitudes and habits that Abram would have to die to. Just like we have to.

When Nancy and I moved to Chicago, it launched her on an unexpected spiritual journey. She loved California so much that she found it hard to find God in Chicago. "It looks like God mashed the whole thing down with an iron," she'd say. Gradually she came to understand that she was in the grips of an idolatry she'd never been warned about: idolatry of place. Going through that open door helped loosen an attachment that kept her from being able to find God anywhere.

At the same time, I had a hard time letting Nancy struggle in our new surroundings. I wanted to either fix her ("Stop whining! Be happy!") or manipulate her ("I guess I made the wrong choice . . . "—not that I thought I had or that I thought she'd think I had, but I thought I might be able to shame her into decreased whining). Going through that open door helped me learn patience and how to offer Nancy the space to be "not okay."

The open door is often more about where my insides are going than where my outsides are going.

God has to begin teaching Abram a whole new way of understanding the world and faith and his own identity. That's why he gives him a new name: "You were Abram, but I will call you Abraham, the father of many nations, because you are to be the man for the world. All the peoples on the earth will be blessed through you" (see Genesis 17:5). God has set before Abram an open door: a new identity, a new faith, a new purpose.

Going through open doors means being willing to leave my idols behind. Abram staying where he was would make that impossible. All his old relationships, all his old patterns, and his old way of life would suck him back into idolatry. Abram would have to leave everything that would keep him from this new life. He would have to go on a journey with God.

What does God give him? A promise. Only a promise: "I will make you into a great nation, and I will bless you; I will make your name great" (Genesis 12:2).

This is a reference to the story of Babel, where human beings say, "We [will] make a name for ourselves" (Genesis 11:4). "We will accomplish impressive achievements so that we are viewed as significant." The God of the open door invites his friends to give up on the project of making their name great, because worth can only be given, never earned.

We waste our whole lives saying, "I will make a name for myself," but God says, "I'm doing something wonderful in the world, and I will give to you what you cannot make for yourself."

Going through open doors will mean I have to trust God with my name.

Open-Door People *Are* Blessed *to* Bless

God tells Abram, "I will make your name great, and you will be a blessing. I will bless those who bless you, and whoever curses you I will curse"—that's a promise of divine protection—"and all peoples on earth will be blessed through you" (Genesis 12:2-3).

But that little word *blessing* needs to be rescued from the clichés of social hashtags. Linguist Deborah Tannen writes, "'Blessed' is used now where in the past one might have said 'lucky.'" Erin Jackson, a stand-up comedian in Virginia, says, "There's literally a chick in my Facebook feed right now who just posted a booty shot of herself—and all it says is 'blessed.' Now wait. Is that really a blessing?" "There's nothing quite like invoking holiness as a way to brag about your life. But calling something 'blessed' has become the go-to term for those who want to boast about an accomplishment while pretending to be humble," observes writer Jessica Bennett.[4]

Blessing, for Abram, was not an opportunity for a social

media "humble brag." ("Can't believe all my herds and flocks and descendants and wives. I'm blessed. #HappyPatriarch.") It was an opportunity to know and experience God, and that included being used by God to enhance others. Abram is called to build his life on this offer: that he can receive a gift from God, but only if he allows his life to become a gift to others.

Trusting in this promise of God leads to a critical dynamic required for open-door thinking. Abram has an attitude of abundance rather than an attitude of scarcity. And that allows him to see and enter the open door of becoming a blessing to others.

When Abram and his nephew Lot separate, Abram allows Lot to choose which land to claim. Lot chooses what looks like the most fertile land ("well watered, like the garden of the LORD"—Genesis 13:10), giving Abram the leftovers. Yet immediately God responds by promising to bless Abram beyond his ability to count.

Later, when Abram meets a mysterious priest-king named Melchizedek, he "gave him a tenth of everything" (Genesis 14:20). Abram invented tithing. Despite Lot's choosing the land "like the garden of the LORD," Abram lived within the promise of God's abundance and blessed others as a result. Going through an open door always requires a spirit of generosity. And generosity flows out of an attitude of abundance, not an attitude of scarcity.

The connection between abundance and blessing rests in God, who combines them both. In the Creation account we're told, "God created the great creatures of the sea and every living thing with which the water teems and that moves about in it. . . . God blessed them and said, 'Be fruitful and increase in number and fill the water in the seas'" (Genesis 1:21-22). "I want lots of you," God says to the fish. "When I look at the water, I want to see fish everywhere."

I love this picture of God blessing fish. How many fish did God make? Many, many fish. "One fish, two fish, red fish, blue fish. . . . Not one of them is like another. Don't ask us why. Go ask your mother."[5] That's why there are so many things: God wants to bless. That means he wants to have things to be able to bless.

This is the *missio Dei*, the mission of God. We talk about mission statements. They go way back before corporations or human organizations. Mission began with God. God has a mission. That's why he made for himself a people, but his mission came before people. His mission came before the Bible. He gave his mission a Bible. He gave his mission a people. God's mission, God's project, is to bless. Open doors are an invitation to be part of the missio Dei.

The reason we love mission statements is we're made in the image of a missional God. His mission is to bless out of his great abundance. And that's your mission too. Just to bless. Where should you do it? Wherever you go. When should you do it? In the words of *Oh, the Places You'll Go!*, "Congratulations! Today is your day."[6]

In Genesis God makes creation in order to have something to bless. Over and over again God blesses, but then sin comes and the curse comes. The word *curse* is used five times in Genesis 3–11 in response to sin; each time it means a loss of freedom and life. Now, in chapter 12, God begins again with this man Abraham, and God uses the word *bless* five times in this passage. He is using one man to reverse the curse.

Blessing in the ancient world was the highest form of well-being possible for human beings. The Greeks referred to the blissful existence of the gods as "blessed." For Israel, blessing included not just gifts from God but especially life with God. Blessing would include all areas of Abram's life: his family, his finances, his work, and his heart. That meant he wasn't just to *receive* a blessing; he was to *be* a blessing. In fact, it is impossible to be blessed in the highest sense apart from becoming a blessing. One of the deepest needs of the human soul is that others should be blessed through our lives. If you want to see the difference between being rich and being blessed, look at Ebenezer Scrooge at the beginning of *A Christmas Carol* and at the end. All the world is to be blessed when Abram goes through this open door—and the world is to be blessed when you and I do as well.

Open-Door People Resist and Persist

Open-door people resist discouragement in the face of obstacles and persist in faithfulness despite long periods of waiting.

God gives Abram a promise: "There's now going to be a 'with-God' people. It's going to happen through you, through a child given to you and Sarai." Abram immediately has good reasons to be skeptical. We've just read this: "Now

Sarai was childless because she was not able to conceive" (Genesis 11:30).

Always in the human soul, there's the potential for this ache around little children. In the ancient world, it was a different deal than it is in our day. Children meant financial security. There was no safety net. There were no pensions or 401(k)s. Children were the continuance of your name. They were a form of immortality. For a woman in particular, in the ancient world, she was understood to be on the planet for the purpose of having children. The inability to bear a child was not just a disappointment; it was a stigma and a shame and a disgrace.

At this point in the account, Abram is seventy-five years old. His wife, Sarai, is sixty-five years old. They have been disappointed with life for a long, long time. They have offered sacrifices to every god they know. They have prayed prayers. Nothing. Now this strange God says, "I'm going to make happen what you've been waiting for, but here's what you have to do. You have to go." How are they going to go? By faith.

The writer of Hebrews says, "By faith Abraham, when called to go to a place he would later receive as his inheritance, obeyed and went, even though he did not know where he was going." You never know where you're going if you're going by faith. "By faith he made his home in the promised land like a stranger in a foreign country" (Hebrews 11:8-9). If you're going by faith, you're always a stranger in this world, because your home is God.

"And by faith even Sarah, who was past childbearing age, was enabled to bear children because she considered him faithful who had made the promise. And so from this one man, and he as good as dead"—don't you love that phrase?—"came descendants as numerous as the stars in the sky and as countless as the sand on the seashore" (Hebrews 11:11-12).

There will always be an excuse to hinder you. Abram's excuse was "I'm too old." It doesn't matter. When you get the divine "go," you resist and persist. You go by faith.

I heard a great line not long ago by a pastor named Craig Groeschel: "If you're not dead, you're not done."

Abram is seventy-five years old. He has to wait another *twenty-four years*. He still doesn't have a child by Sarai when God comes to him again twenty-four years later and repeats the promise, and here's his response: "Abraham fell facedown; he laughed and said to himself, 'Will a son be born to a man a hundred years old? Will Sarah bear a child at the age of ninety?'" (Genesis 17:17).

"Sarah will bear you a son," God responds (Genesis 17:19). "I don't care how old she is." If you're not dead, you're not done. "In fact," God says, "Abraham, I will now give you a sign of my promise, of my covenant, because I want you to put your faith not in your own wisdom, not in your ability to know what's going on or to predict the future or to foresee circumstances or to engineer outcomes. I want you to put all of your trust in me, in life with me."

If you're not dead, you're not done. In the Bible, age is never a reason for someone to say no when God says go.

Moses is eighty years old when God calls him to go to Pharaoh and lead the children of Israel out of Egypt. The Exodus *starts* when he's eighty. Caleb is eighty when he asks God to give him one more mountain to take in the Promised Land.

Florence Detlor, a woman at the church where I work, decided a few years ago that she needed a new challenge, so she went on Facebook.

She was 101 years old at the time.

It turns out that out of the one billion or so people who were on Facebook, Florence Detlor was the oldest. In fact, when Mark Zuckerberg found out, he invited Florence Detlor from our church to go to Facebook headquarters on a personal tour and have her picture taken with him and Sheryl Sandberg.

When the first television interview went public, in a single day Florence got seven thousand friend requests. Seven thousand people from around the world said, "Florence, would you be my friend?" She says she's getting carpal tunnel syndrome trying to respond to requests for her friendship—at the age of 101. If you're not dead, you're not done.

Abraham tried to say no because he was too old. Timothy tried to say no because he was too young. Esther tried to say no because she was the wrong gender. Moses tried to say no because he had the wrong gifts. Gideon tried to say no because he was from the wrong tribe. Elijah tried to say no because he had the wrong enemy. Jonah tried to say no because he was sent to the wrong city. Paul tried to say no because he had the wrong background. God kept saying, "Go, go. *You* go." Sometimes it takes a while for God's promises to be fulfilled. But if you're not dead, that's the clue you're not done.

Open-Door People Have Fewer Regrets

Some of the saddest stories are about calls that never get answered, risks that never get taken, obedience that never gets offered, joyful generosity that never gets given, adventures that never happen, lives that never get lived. I hope that's not you.

There is an entire field of study in the social sciences around the psychology of regret. One of the most striking findings is the way that regret changes over the course of our lives. Short-term regrets most often involve wishing we hadn't done something: I wish I hadn't eaten that peach cobbler. I wish I hadn't asked that girl out and been rejected.

The world of social media even has an acronym for this one: YOLO—"you only live once." This is associated with the reckless pursuit of fun while throwing off the consequences of reason and responsibility. It is most often used when you choose the unfortunate option. "Who knew the highway patrol was so picky about texting while doing 85 mph?—YOLO."

But over time, our perspective shifts. As we get older, we come to regret those actions that we *did not take.* The word of love we never spoke. The chance to serve we never took. The costly gift we never gave.

We begin our lives regretting the wrong things we have done, but we end them regretting the open doors we never went through. What do we need to do now so that we're not living in regret then? Walking through open doors keeps us from future regrets. We may have short-term regrets if we make the wrong choice, but going through open doors keeps us from wondering what might have been.

The divine "go" comes into every life, but we must be willing to leave before we're willing to go.

As I was reading Abram's story, I wondered, *What if this story had taken place today? In our world, what land is known for its great concentration of wealth, technology, mobility, education, and learning?*

And then it dawned on me: I live in Ur of the Chaldeans. I live in a place that takes great pride in its wealth and technology and education. I can begin to build my identity and esteem around that. Maybe you can too.

What do we say when the divine "go" comes to us?

If I go, I might mess up, but if I don't go, if I don't risk, if I don't try, if I don't say yes, I will never do something wonderful for God. If I say yes, I might fail, but if I don't, I will never get to the promised land of life with God to be a blessing in his world.

There's this very intriguing little detail in the text about Abram's dad: "Terah took his son Abram, his grandson Lot son of Haran, and his daughter-in-law Sarai, the wife of his son Abram, and together they set out from Ur of the Chaldeans to go to Canaan. But when they came to Harran, they settled there" (Genesis 11:31). Terah accompanied Abram for part of the journey to Canaan, but then he stopped.

We don't know for sure—the passage doesn't give many details—but here's what may have been going on. Terah and his family begin their story in Ur, the great center of wealth and education and the land of idols. Then they begin on this road, which passes through the city of Harran and then down into Canaan. But we're told that for Terah, the father of Abram, the road ends in Harran. Now we know from other passages in the Bible that Harran was a city a lot like Ur. There was a lot of wealth there. There were idols there.

What's going on? We don't know for sure, but we do know from the text that Terah sets out for Canaan, but when he gets to a place that's a lot like Ur, he settles there. He never goes on.

Maybe God said to Terah, "Oh, the places you'll go!" but Terah said, "No, I don't think so. I think I'll stop here."

It may well be that what's going on here is that Terah thinks to himself, *If I were to go any farther than this, I could lose everything I have. For sure, I would have to give up my idols.* So he chooses comfort. But Abram chooses to say yes to his calling.

Into your life will come a divine "go," but you live in Ur of the Chaldeans, and you'll have to decide between comfort and calling. Terah is a picture of what might be called the road not taken.

I wonder if Terah regretted staying in the safety and comfort of Harran. Imagine that you are Terah. Imagine that you lived to be very old and found out that God's story went on in remarkable ways and that your grandson Isaac, the child named Laughter, was the promise of God fulfilled. Would you be sorry that you chose comfort over calling? Unlike Terah, Abram has many mistakes recorded in Scripture. But unlike Abram, Terah is never called a friend of God. Perhaps open-door people make more mistakes but have fewer regrets.

A few months into our marriage, while I was still in grad school, I got a phone call telling me I was being offered a fellowship to study overseas for a year. I told Nancy and then asked a series of questions. Would the classes count toward my degree? (No.) Would it take me longer to graduate if we went? (Yes.) Would there be enough money to travel on? (No.) Would anyone at the school be waiting for us? (No.) Would Nancy have to work? (Yes. As a maid.)

I hung up the phone, thinking Nancy and I had a lot of pros and cons to weigh about this decision. But when I went in to talk with her about the details, I found that she had already packed.

That's when I realized I was married to a woman of the open door. Her default is set to yes.

God is doing something magnificent in this world. When a door is opened, count the costs, weigh the pros and cons, get wise counsel, look as far down the road as you can. But in your deepest heart, in its most secret place, have a tiny bias in the direction of *yes*. Cultivate a *willingness* to charge through open doors even if it's not this particular door.

God came to Abram and said, "I will bless you. I will

make your name great. I'll make you a great people. I'll protect you. All the peoples on the earth will be blessed through you."

Pause.

What did Abram do?

Abram went.

Terah settled; Abram went.

God said, "Go"; Abram said yes.

And that was enough for God, even though he knew Abram would not always get things perfect.

Open-Door People Learn about Themselves

If I am to go through open doors, I will have to trust that God can use me in spite of my imperfections. I will learn about myself, warts and all, in ways that I never would have otherwise.

When I go through open doors, I will often discover that my faith is really weaker than I thought it was before I went through. If I am to go through open doors, I will have to be humble enough to accept failure.

A classic example of this happens when Israel escapes from slavery in Egypt. After Moses meets God in the burning bush, he and Aaron gather the Israelite slaves to tell them what God has said and show them miraculous signs, "and they believed. And when they heard that the LORD was concerned about them and had seen their misery, they bowed down and worshiped" (Exodus 4:31).

They hear. They believe.

Shortly after this, just as they are leaving Egypt, they see Pharaoh coming after them. They say to Moses, "Was it because there were no graves in Egypt that you brought us to the desert to die? What have you done to us by bringing us out of Egypt? Didn't we say to you in Egypt, 'Leave us alone; let us serve the Egyptians'?" (Exodus 14:11-12).

Did they say that in Egypt? No! In Egypt they said, "We believe."

When they said that, they were sincere. But that belief turned out to be fickle. When their circumstances changed, it turned out they didn't *really* believe at all.

We do this all the time. For example, if you ask me, I'll tell you I believe in a marriage of equal servanthood, where husbands and wives equally share division of labor. In reality (want to guess where this is headed?), I often find myself doing far *more* than my fair share around the house and robbing my spouse of her opportunity to serve.

I also lie a lot.

Or, for another example, consider my relationship with money. Jesus said, "It is more blessed to give than to receive. Don't be anxious about possessions or money; trust your Father in heaven." I think, *That's what I believe. I don't trust in money.* But then, if I actually go through a door of generous or sacrificial giving, if the economy dips, or if I suddenly have less money, I get anxious, stressed, and worried.

Turns out I believe I don't trust in money—as long as I *have* money. But when I lose some—keeping in mind that even then, I'm still not going to starve and I'm still better off than most in the world—my *real* beliefs are revealed. Apparently I *do* trust in money. A lot.

When I walk through an open door, I often learn truths about myself that I would never have learned if I'd stayed on the other side.

Open-Door People Are Not Paralyzed by Their Imperfection

We have a tendency to view the people who walk through God's open doors as spiritual giants, possessing a faith we could never possibly reach. But there's a fabulous insight to be gained when we look at the remarkable words Paul uses to describe Abraham:

> Against all hope, Abraham in hope believed and so became the father of many nations, just as it had been said to him. . . . Without weakening in his faith, he faced the fact that his body was as good as dead— since he was about a hundred years old—and that Sarah's womb was also dead. Yet he did not waver through unbelief regarding the promise of God, but was strengthened in his faith and gave glory to God, being fully persuaded that God had power to do what he had promised. (Romans 4:18-21)

Paul presents Abraham as one who believed God, "and it was credited to him as righteousness" (Romans 4:22). Another way of saying this is that God chose to work with

Abraham on the basis of Abraham's willingness to trust him rather than Abraham's always having done the right thing. And it turns out that when you read Abraham's story, even his belief in God looks pretty ragged.

As soon as Abram pulls the family together to obey God's call, they travel to Egypt, and Abram says to his wife, "You're a beautiful woman; I'm afraid the Egyptians will want to kill me so someone can have you for a wife, so let's lie and tell them you're my sister."

He doesn't seem very confident that God will protect him. (Plus, Sarai was sixty-five at the time.) He throws his wife under the bus.

Pharaoh *does* take Sarai into his palace to join the harem—giving Abram her "brother" a bunch of sheep, cattle, donkeys, servants, and camels. Rather than feeling guilty and coming clean, Abram simply says, "Thank you very much."

Then Pharaoh finds out that Sarai is actually Abram's wife and that Abram's God is not happy about this arrangement. It's interesting that Pharaoh asks Abram the same question in the same language that God used when he addressed Eve after the Fall: "What have you done?" (Genesis 12:18; see Genesis 3:13). In other words, this pagan Pharaoh is more concerned about doing what is right than God's man Abram.

And not only that, but when Abram and Sarai are in the Negev later in Genesis, he does the whole "she's my sister" routine a *second time.*

Why doesn't God just give up on him?

Because, as we'll see, the one thing Abram gets right is

that he doesn't give up on God. Perhaps God will keep the door of opportunity open for us as we keep the door of our heart open to him.

When God still hasn't provided the promised child after eleven years of waiting, Sarai says to Abram, "Why don't you go ahead and have a child with my servant Hagar?"

Does Abram say, "Heaven forbid! Let's trust God"?

No. He says, "Well, honey, whatever you say." It's a train wreck.

And when God shows up three years later to tell Abraham that Sarah will have a baby, what is his reaction? "Abraham fell facedown; he laughed and said to himself, 'Will a son be born to a man a hundred years old?'" (Genesis 17:17).

Not only that, Sarah laughs when she hears the news. So the Lord asks Abraham, "Why did Sarah laugh . . . ? Is anything too hard for the LORD?" (Genesis 18:13-14).

Does Abraham man up and say, "Well, Lord, to tell you the truth, I got a chuckle out of it myself"?

No. He says nothing.

He has so little faith that he pretends Sarah is not his wife—twice; so little faith that he impregnates a servant girl; so little faith that he laughs under his breath at God's promise. And *this* is the man about whom Paul says "against all hope, Abraham in hope believed," "without weakening," "did not waver through unbelief," "was strengthened in his faith," "[was] fully persuaded that God had power"?

And Paul was a rabbi. Paul knew the story. So why his lavish praise for Abraham?

Let's go back and enter Abraham's world. When Abraham said yes to God, he was starting from scratch. There was no Old Testament. How many of the Ten Commandments did Abraham know? None! There was no law, no Temple, no priests. No psalms, no David, no Moses. He had heard exactly zero information about Yahweh. He was the product of a brutal, superstitious culture.

Here's the key: "So Abram went, as the LORD had told him" (Genesis 12:4).

The Scriptures deliberately do not present Abraham as a brilliant spiritual genius who innovated the concept of ethical monotheism. He was full of ignorance, uncertainty, mistakes, and cowardice.

Why was his faith regarded as strong? Because he chose to wait for a son only God could bring.

He was not in denial. "He faced the fact that his body was as good as dead" (Romans 4:19). He was an old man with an old wife and an old body and no pharmaceutical companies to help him out.

Abraham did not allow his life to be determined by what is possible through merely human power. He left when God said, "Go." He went on a journey that could be successful only if God honored his word. In that way—and perhaps *only* in that way—Abraham truly depended on God.

The story does *not* depend on Abraham's certainty. He did not say, "Sarah, we just have to *believe God* for this baby. We just have to *claim* the promise."

The hero of this story isn't Abraham. It's God.

Terah might have had much stronger faith than his son Abraham—but he put it in the wrong place. Even though Abraham made a lot of mistakes along the way, he got the main thing right: he didn't go back to Ur. He went where God told him to go.

It's better to have little faith in a big God than to have big faith in a little god. That's why Jesus said we just need faith like a mustard seed.

I once heard pastor and author Tim Keller speaking about the Israelites' escape from Egypt. As Pharaoh came after them, God parted the Red Sea, and the Israelites crossed over on dry ground. Most likely some of them were reveling in it: "In your face, Pharaoh! We're cruising now!"

But at the same time, others were probably saying, "We're all gonna die! We're all gonna die!"

It's not the *quality* of our faith that saves us, Tim said. It's the *object* of our faith.

This is why Paul wedges in this description of the God Abraham believed in: "[Abraham] is our father in the sight of God, in whom he believed—the God who gives life to the dead and calls into being things that were not" (Romans 4:17). The character of Abraham's faith is determined by the character of the God in whom he believed.[7]

It turns out you don't YOLO after all. The only thing God needed to get this redemption project going was Abraham's trust. Not perfection. Not superhuman efforts. Simple trust. God can work with that.

The worst year in my life was maybe the best in my wife's.

I had lived for many months with a deep depression and a feeling of pain that would not go away. It seemed clear to me that my life's work would continually be less effective. At the same time, Nancy had taken a new full-time job and was soaring with a level of energy and joy I had never seen in her before.

I can remember lying in bed at night, listening to her having meetings downstairs in our home with the staff she led, hearing laughter and enthusiasm and planning happening recreationally—and being thoroughly miserable. Her energized success made my own painful inadequacy look that much darker. I found myself quite envious.

One night while I was wrestling with this, a question entered my mind: *Do I want to be the kind of man who needs his wife to be less successful so he can feel better about himself?*

I lay still for several minutes, hoping for an easier question.

But I knew the answer. Many things were unclear to me, but I knew I did not want to be the kind of person who needs his spouse to look smaller so he can feel bigger.

And in a strange way, seeing that weakness and neediness in myself was the beginning of healing. Ernest Kurtz writes in *The Spirituality of Imperfection* that, ironically, perfectionism is the great enemy of spiritual growth. An ancient sage named Macarius used to point out that if all we did was make progress, we would become conceited, and conceit is the ultimate downfall of Christians.

Maybe part of why God lets us see so clearly the imperfections of the characters in the Bible is so that we can more clearly recognize our own. In one Hasidic story a man of great wealth visits a rabbi and confesses that secretly, despite his riches, he is miserable. The rabbi asks him what he sees when he looks out the window, and the man tells him, "People. People walking by."

Then the rabbi asks what he sees in the mirror, and the man says, "I see myself."

"Perhaps that is the problem," the rabbi says. "Notice that in the window there is glass, and in the mirror there is glass. But as soon as a little silver is added, you cease to see others and see only yourself."[8]

God begins the redemption project with a call to imperfect Abraham. And then there's Isaac, and then Jacob, and eventually fishermen and tax collectors and lepers and prostitutes.

Sometimes people answered the call and walked through the open door. And when they did, they got to be part of the story. Sometimes people said no, as was the case with the Rich Young Ruler. When Jesus said, "Go, sell everything you have. Then come and follow me," the man went away sad, because he lived in Ur of the Chaldeans and his idol was money. He just couldn't bring himself to walk through the divine door.

It all began with the opportunity in front of Abraham: "Go, and all the peoples of the earth will be blessed." And it continued right through to Jesus: "Go and make disciples of all the peoples of the earth, be their name 'Buxbaum or Bixby or Bray or Mordecai Ali Van Allen O'Shea.' At last, all these years after Abraham, all the nations will be blessed. 'Kid, you'll move mountains!'"[9]

Dr. Seuss, by the way, didn't invent that idea of moving mountains. Jesus said, "If you have faith as small as a mustard seed, you can say to this mountain, 'Move from here to there,' and it will move" (Matthew 17:20). It's not the quality of our faith; it's the object of our faith.

At the end of his ministry, before he ascended into heaven, Jesus said to his students, to his graduates (I understand this is not actually in the book, that Matthew forgot to write it down, but I'm pretty sure what got said was this): "Oh, the places you'll go! You'll travel the world. You'll stand before kings. You'll have absolutely no money and be outrageously happy. You'll be locked up in prison, and you'll sing songs. You'll be beaten for your faith and count yourself honored to have suffered for the name. You'll have nothing. You'll have no 401(k)s, you'll have no IRAs, you'll have no health care, and you will trust me down to the absolute core of your being."

Then Jesus invited them to go, as Jesus invites us still, because this is his mission.

Because one day before all of eternity, the Father called the Son to go: "Son, you're going to leave heaven. You will go to a manger, and you will go to a little carpenter's shop, and you're going to flee to Egypt as a fugitive.

"You're going to go to banquets no other rabbi would ever go to with tax collectors and prostitutes, and you're going to go to houses where they make holes in the roof just to get down to you because they're so excited you've come. You're going to go to where lepers are. You're going to go to the crippled. You're going to go to the blind. You're going to go to the impoverished. You're going to go to the sin-soaked and the hopeless.

"Then one day, Son, you're going to go to a cross, and you're going to bleed, and you're going to die to forgive the sins of the world. Then you're going to go to the tomb, but then, Son, death is going to find out it can't hold you and can't stop you.

"And on the third day the stone will be rolled away, and you're going to bring joy to the world as far as the curse is found."

He still calls. He still sends.

And if you say yes . . .

Oh, the places you'll go.

CHAPTER 3

NO MO FOMO: OVERCOMING THE FEAR OF MISSING OUT

A NUMBER OF STUDIES have shown that going on Facebook tends to depress people.[1] We often want to use our Facebook profile to enhance our image, to post pictures that make us look more attractive than we really are, and to list accomplishments and omit failures in order to boost our self-esteem. (Ironically it's vulnerability, not invincibility, that leads to the human connections we really hunger for. Maybe we would be better served by "Fall Flat on Your Face-Book.")

We become curators of our own selves, but it turns out that going on Facebook makes us more likely to end up envying others and feeling diminished worth.

It got me thinking. What if God were on Facebook? What would his page look like? And what if he approached his profile the way most of us do?

The Deity
Relationship status: Triune and serenely blissful
Number of friends: God only knows
Unfriended: List currently blocked
Photos: None available (see second commandment)
Timeline: Saturday, October 22, 4004 BC—Created
 the world . . . or did I?
What's on your mind?: What isn't?
Recent posts:
- I rule!
- I'm thinking about writing another book—my first one is still the all-time bestseller and the bestseller every year.
- Now have over one billion worshipers. What ever happened to Zeus?
- Taking the day off. Thank me it's Friday!

Thank God that when he became visible, the face we saw was Jesus, who humbled himself and served others. Thank God that we are called to seek his face and not his Facebook.

It turns out that this epidemic of comparing our lives to

others' that social media has escalated has led to a new electronically spread disease. Sherry Turkle, a professor at MIT, calls it FOMO: fear of missing out.

We're afraid that other people are doing more interesting things than we're doing, or making more friends than we're making, or discovering better ways of getting in shape or saving money or managing their emotions than we are. A recent bestseller by Mindy Kaling has a vividly FOMO title: *Is Everyone Hanging Out without Me?* We're afraid there's something wonderful going on somewhere and we're missing out. Have we taken the wrong job or connected with the wrong people or made the wrong commitment or chosen the wrong event?

We're afraid we're missing out on our children growing up. Afraid we're missing out on what could be great careers. Afraid we're missing out on financial opportunities other people are grabbing, or great vacations other people are taking, or wonderful abilities other people are acquiring.

We keep reading online about the wonderful experiences our friends or others are having, sometimes in real time, and are increasingly afraid that our lives are dull and insignificant by comparison. One way we cope with that is by posting pictures and experiences that make our own lives sound more glamorous than they really are, which in turn makes other people fear that *they* are missing out.

It's worse now because we have more choices than ever. If you're under thirty, there's a good chance you'll have a job one day that hasn't even been invented yet. It's worse now because we have more opportunity than ever to compare ourselves to others, and FOMO is often fed by comparison. But here's some good advice: "Never compare your behind-the-scenes with everyone else's highlight reel."[2]

FOMO, in a way, is behind the very first sin. The serpent asks Eve, "Did God really say, 'You must not eat from any tree?' . . . God knows that when you eat from it your eyes will be opened, and you will be like God" (Genesis 3:1, 5). Cain and Abel, Jacob and Esau, Rachel and Leah, and David and Bathsheba are all stories of sin driven by FOMO.

And yet, for all of its dangers, FOMO tells us something fundamental about ourselves. We have an insatiable hunger for more. We have a longing for life beyond what we are experiencing right now. Handled rightly, FOMO can lead us toward God's open doors.

The apostle Paul sat in chains, imprisoned, and wrote of a God beyond our imagining:

> Now to him who is able to do immeasurably more
> than all we ask or imagine, according to his power
> that is at work within us, to him be glory in the
> church and in Christ Jesus throughout all generations,
> for ever and ever! Amen. (Ephesians 3:20-21)

God is able to do what we ask.
God is able to do what we ask *and what we imagine.*
God is able to do *all* we ask and imagine.
God is able to do *more than* all we ask and imagine.

God is able to do *immeasurably* more than all we ask or imagine.

That's God.

Fear of missing out is behind the appeal of the greatest creative genius in American history. I refer not to Walt Disney or Steve Jobs or Thomas Edison but rather to Ron Popeil, the founder of Ronco who thought up the Veg-O-Matic, Dial-O-Matic, Dice-O-Matic, Bass-O-Matic, and the amazing hair in a can, as well as a hundred other inventions that have changed people's lives. But his greatest creation isn't any of those. It's the tagline that invariably popped up in his late-night infomercials: "But wait! There's more." No matter how wonderful the last appliance, no matter how tantalizing the last offer, the human imagination is always fired up by that one promise:

But wait! There's more.

Cheryl Forbes once said people who live imaginative lives are *what-if?* people. They respond to ideas and events with a *what-if?* attitude. They behave in *what-if?* ways. *What if?* is a big idea, as big as God, for it is the practice of God. Our God thinks, *What if I make a universe? What if I make people in my own image? What if, when they sin, I don't give up on them?*

Jesus comes to people and invites us to be *what-if?* people. He said to his early followers, "I want you to imagine a kingdom—the *real* magic kingdom. Imagine a kingdom where the last are first, the least are greatest, the servants are heroes, the weak are strong, and the marginalized are loved and cherished. Imagine a world where outsiders become insiders, where people who lose their lives end up finding them, where people who die to themselves and their guilt and their sin and their selfishness end up being brought to life. Imagine that your little broken story can become part of a larger story that ends well."

Then in the most unimaginable moment in human history, Jesus said to himself, *What if I die on a cross and take on myself all that sin and all that suffering and all that pain and all that guilt and all that death that now crushes the human race?* And he did it. They put his body in a tomb, and three days later God said to Jesus, "Now what if you get up?" He got up, and death has never been the same. *Life* has never been the same.

After he got up from that grave, he gathered eleven un-educated, unconnected, unresourced followers and said, "But wait! There's more. There's more than life, and there's more than death. What if I were to tell you that in addition to this matchless teaching I've been giving you, beyond the forgive-ness of your sins, I'm going to throw in a new community of brothers and sisters that'll be like a family to you?

"Imagine you're going to be given the Holy Spirit to lead and guide you all together. You're going to be sent out, scattered all over the world. Eventually, you'll be killed. Of course, death can't stop your existence with God, and it can't stop this dream. This movement, this community, is just going to keep spreading until it reaches more people in more places, embraces more cultures, and shapes more lives than any movement in human history."

Then he did that. It actually happened, and here we are. Faith is, among other things, an act of the imagination. The Bible says, "Now faith is confidence in what we hope for and assurance about what we do not see" (Hebrews 11:1). That means God is still looking for *what-if?* people because . . . Wait! There's more.

The real, deep reason that FOMO exists is that we *were* made for more and we *are* missing out. Only the "more" isn't more money or more success or more impressive experiences I can write about on Facebook. My hunger for more turns out to be insatiable if I try to satisfy it by wanting more for *me*.

This brings us to one of the most important features of open doors in the Bible. Biblically speaking, open doors are divine invitations to make our lives count, with God's help, for the sake of others. If I forget "for the sake of others," my search for open doors turns into one more doomed attempt at an impressive Facebook post. Frederick Buechner writes, "To journey for the sake of saving our own lives is little by little to cease to live in any sense that really matters, even to ourselves, because it is only by journeying for the world's sake—even when the world bores and sickens and scares you half to death—that little by little we start to come alive."[3]

"More," if it's only more for *me*, turns out to be less. Narcissus was looking for a mirror, not an open door. The secret of the open door is that it appears most often when we stop obsessing over self-advancement and look instead for opportunities to love.

Which brings us to a woman named Ruth.

Love Finds Doors That Ambition Never Could

"In the days when the judges ruled, there was a famine in the land" (Ruth 1:1).

In the middle of the famine, there's this little family—Elimelek and Naomi and their two sons, Mahlon and Kilion—and they're going to starve. So they leave their home, and they go to a land called Moab.

The Moabites were the great enemies of Israel. They were pagans. They worshiped idols. The Moabites were not even allowed to go to the Temple and worship in Israel. So an Israelite reading this story knew it would be a broken story. This was a bad situation. Nobody liked the Moabites.

After ten years in exile in this bad country, the father and both of the sons in the family die. Naomi is left a widow in exile with no husband, no sons, and no grandchildren who will care for her as she grows old. Her husband's name—*Elimelek*—means "God is king." If God is king, he has a strange way of ruling.

Then there's a small turn in the story: "When Naomi heard in Moab that the LORD had come to the aid of his people by providing food for them, she and her daughters-in-law prepared to return home from there" (Ruth 1:6).

There is the hint of a tiny open door.

Naomi's daughters-in-law, Orpah and Ruth, are going with her. They leave the little town where they live in Moab, and they hit the road. But when they get out of town, Naomi stops and says to the girls, "Go back, each of you, to your mother's home. May the LORD show you kindness, as you have shown kindness to your dead husbands and to me. May the LORD grant that each of you will find rest in the home of another husband" (Ruth 1:8-9). After this speech, she kisses the girls, and they all cry.

This is a really poignant scene. Naomi has nothing left to give her daughters-in-law. She has no money and no connections. She can't help them. The only thing she can give them is freedom from the burden of having to care for her. So that's what she gives them. She says, "You'll have a better chance to find a husband if you stay here." In that culture, getting married wasn't just about romance. It was survival. It was economic well-being.

The girls, amazingly, refuse to obey. They say, "Nope. We're going to stay with you," even though Naomi can't help them at all. She's going to be a burden to them.

So Naomi tries again. "Return home, my daughters. . . . I am too old to have another husband. Even if I thought there was still hope for me—even if I had a husband tonight and then gave birth to sons—would you wait until they grew up?" (Ruth 1:11-13). In the ancient world, the idea was that if your husband died, maybe the family who gave you that husband would replace him. But Naomi is walking the girls through her situation. "Even if I could help you there, it would take too long."

Naomi continues, "'No, my daughters. It is more bitter for me than for you, because the LORD's hand has turned against me!' At this they wept aloud again. Then Orpah kissed her mother-in-law goodbye, but Ruth clung to her" (Ruth 1:13-14).

Notice there are two daughters-in-law in this situation. Two doors: one marked Stay and one marked Leave. Two young women: one named Ruth and one named Orpah. One of them, Orpah, listens to Naomi. Orpah goes back home. Orpah stays in Moab. We don't hear from Orpah again until many years later when she becomes a famous television talk show host.

But Ruth won't go back to Moab. Naomi tries again. "'Look,' said Naomi, 'your sister-in-law is going back to her people and her gods. Go back with her'" (Ruth 1:15). Four times in this short passage Naomi says to Ruth, "Go back," and Ruth stands in the valley of decision. Now her destiny will be determined. From this young woman—this destitute, penniless, pagan Moabite widow—comes one of the great statements of devotion in all of human literature, let alone in all the Bible:

> Don't urge me to leave you or to turn back from you. Where you go I will go, and where you stay I will stay. Your people will be my people and your God my God. Where you die I will die, and there I will be buried. May the LORD deal with me, be it ever so severely, if even death separates you and me. (Ruth 1:16-17)

Unbelievable devotion, almost without precedent.

Two characters, two daughters-in-law, Orpah and Ruth. Orpah does what is prudent, expedient, expected, and rational. The Bible doesn't criticize her for this. Not at all. She does what any reasonable person would do. She makes a reasonable choice. She lives a reasonable life. Ruth does what only an unreasonable person would do. Ruth decides to live an unreasonable life.

God didn't ask her to do this; she just chose, and now she'll be living in the Kingdom in partnership with God. Now amazing things will happen to her—but she doesn't know that when she makes her choice. She just bets everything she has on love.

I wonder what you're choosing. I know we live in a society that will tell you, "Be reasonable. Be prudent. Build a successful career. Be secure. Use all your time and energy and resources." You can do that if you want to—great résumé, great benefits—or you can bet everything on love.

When the Jesuit order began, they chose as their motto a single word that their founder, Ignatius, used to inspire heroic deeds: *magis*, the Latin word for "more." This simple motto captured "a broader spirit, a restless drive to imagine whether there isn't some even greater project to be accomplished or some better way of attacking the current problem." Loyola himself described the ideal Jesuit as living "with one foot raised"—always ready to go through the open door. By 1800 it is estimated that one-fifth of Europe was educated by Jesuit-led schools.[4] We were made for "more"; not to *have* more out of love for self, but to *do* more out of love for God.

But wait! There's *magis*.

It doesn't have to look big.

I watch Hank, a brilliant businessman, rearrange his life when his wife is diagnosed with Parkinson's disease. Hours that were once devoted to issuing directives and generating massive revenues are now spent helping wheel his wife in her chair to settings that will bring her joy. I watch Sarah graduate from an elite school and choose to devote her time to helping young students in a volunteer organization where she'll have to raise her own meager support. Every day unsung heroes among us sacrifice themselves to care for aging parents or children with Down syndrome or parentless gang members. It often looks as though they have sacrificed the adventure of opportunities for this. But what if . . .

"When Naomi saw that [Ruth] was determined to go with her, she said no more to her" (Ruth 1:18, NRSV). They just walked the road together. It's remarkable. This is quite unusual, maybe unprecedented in ancient literature. This is a road story about a buddy relationship, only it's two women instead of two men. They're taking on the world. This is Thelma and Louise, headed from Moab to Israel together. Live or die, it's the two of them to the end of the road.

Ruth has no idea, but the choice she made is going to open a door for her to become part of a story larger than she dreams. Her name will be remembered for millennia. She will become a role model and a prayer: "May you be like Ruth and like Esther." But she did not choose to go with Naomi for any of those reasons. She just chose the opportunity to love.

Actually Noticing People Leads to Doors

In the second chapter of the story, Ruth and Naomi are in Israel. "Ruth the Moabite said to Naomi, 'Let me go to the fields and pick up the leftover grain behind anyone in whose eyes I find favor'" (Ruth 2:2). In the first chapter, when they are in Moab, she is simply "Ruth." But now she's a foreigner, different, "other"—"Ruth *the Moabite*."

She goes into the field of Boaz, and as it happens, he's actually a distant relative of Naomi's, so maybe he will care about Naomi's situation. And he does. Now the door of God's favor begins to open for Ruth. Boaz hears the story of what Ruth is doing, and he's moved by her character. So he calls Ruth aside and says, "You just glean in my fields when you come out every day. I've given my men instructions not to lay a hand on you. I know a poor, powerless widow could be vulnerable, so I've told those guys to be nice."

He says, "When you're thirsty because it's hot and this is hard work, I've told the guys to give you water to drink." It's touching thoughtfulness on Boaz's part. In the ancient world, and in a lot of the two-thirds world today, drawing water is really hard work, and it's usually a woman's job. Women commonly have to get water not just for themselves but for the men working in the field, or wherever they are working. Boaz says, "I've told my guys not only do *you* not have to draw water for *them*, *they* have to draw water for *you*, a foreign widow."

Because Ruth has been kind to Naomi, she unwittingly sets in motion a chain of events where Boaz is going to be kind to her. Throughout this story, the opportunity to do kindness to someone who is "foreign" transcends the boundaries that would normally separate people and causes them to see each other in a new light. Doors open when I actually notice and care about people I might otherwise overlook.

I read about a woman who locked her keys in her car in a rough neighborhood. She tried a coat hanger to break into her car, but she couldn't get that to work. Finally, she prayed, "God, send me somebody to help me." Five minutes later, a rusty old car pulled up. A tattooed, bearded man wearing a biker's skull rag walked toward her. She thought, *God, really? Him?* But she was desperate.

So when the man asked if he could help, she said, "Can you break into my car?" He said, "Not a problem." He took the coat hanger and opened the car in a few seconds. She said to him, "You're a very nice man" and gave him a big hug. He said, "I'm not a nice man. I just got out of prison today. I served two years for auto theft, and I've only been out a couple of hours." She hugged him again and shouted, "Thank you, God, for sending me a professional!"

When I look for God's open doors, I begin to see even the mundane circumstances of my life as an opportunity to serve others. There was a front-page article in the *San Francisco Chronicle* about a metro-transit operator named Linda Wilson-Allen.[5] She loves the people who ride her bus. She knows the regulars. She learns their names. She will wait for them if they're late and then make up the time later on her route.

A woman in her eighties named Ivy had some heavy grocery bags and was struggling with them. So Linda got out of her bus driver's seat to carry Ivy's grocery bags onto the bus. Now Ivy lets other buses pass her stop so she can ride on Linda's bus.

Linda saw a woman named Tanya in a bus shelter. She could tell Tanya was new to the area. She could tell she was lost. It was almost Thanksgiving, so Linda said to Tanya, "You're out here all by yourself. You don't know anybody. Come on over for Thanksgiving and kick it with me and the kids." Now they're friends.

The reporter who wrote the article rides Linda's bus every day. He said Linda has built such a little community of blessing on that bus that passengers offer Linda the use of their vacation homes. They bring her potted plants and floral bouquets. When people found out she likes to wear scarves to accessorize her uniforms, they started giving them as presents to Linda. One passenger upgraded her gift to a rabbit-fur collar. The article says Linda may be the most beloved bus driver since Ralph Kramden on *The Honeymooners*. (Does anybody remember old Ralph Kramden?)

Think about what a thankless task driving a bus can look like in our world: cranky passengers, engine breakdowns, traffic jams, gum on the seats. You ask yourself, *How does she have this attitude?* "Her mood is set at 2:30 a.m. when she gets down on her knees to pray for 30 minutes," the *Chronicle* says. "'There is a lot to talk about with the Lord,' says Wilson-Allen, a member of Glad Tidings Church in Hayward."

When she gets to the end of her line, she always says, "That's all. I love you. Take care." Have you ever had a bus driver tell you, "I love you"? People wonder, *Where can I find the Kingdom of God?* I will tell you where. You can find it on the #45 bus riding through San Francisco. People wonder, *Where can I find the church?* I will tell you. Behind the wheel of a metro transit vehicle.

We invited Linda to speak at our church. People with all kinds of Silicon Valley dreams were inspired to standing ovations by a woman who drives a bus. They stood in line by the dozens afterward to talk with her. For the door on the #45 bus opens into the Kingdom of God.

Open doors are everywhere, every day. And when we follow God's leading, we receive the blessing of seeing the world and our place in it as he sees it.

Open Doors Lead to Relational Intimacy

Naomi, when she hears about Boaz's kindness, is really struck by it, and she gets this idea. She thinks, *Maybe there's more than just compassion and generosity going on in Boaz's heart.* So she tells Ruth, "I want you to go back to Boaz. This time go to him at night." Then she says to Ruth, "Wash, put on perfume, and get dressed in your best clothes" (Ruth 3:3).

Naomi is giving Ruth dating advice. Remember, there were no articles about dating in the time of the judges. Orpah hadn't started her magazine yet, so advice had to travel just by word of mouth. Ruth follows Naomi's suggestions, and using the symbolism of her day, she invites Boaz at night to cover her with his cloak. It is a really tender, kind of charged scene.

Ruth is essentially proposing to Boaz. She knows that since Boaz is a relative of Naomi, if Boaz cares for her, Naomi is going to be cared for also. Boaz understands this, and he's immensely moved. He says to Ruth, "This kindness is greater than that which you showed earlier: You have not run after the younger men, whether rich or poor" (Ruth 3:10). The idea here is not that Boaz is some old goat. Extreme modesty was considered polite in the ancient Near East, so it would be typical for the man to say, "You could have had far more handsome men than me." Then the woman would be expected to say, "No, you're way more handsome than what I ever thought I would get." There's that kind of deal going on here.

This is just a beautiful story. Part of what's beautiful about it is that Ruth and Boaz are drawn to each other's character. Physical attraction is a gift, but when you're looking for a spouse, there ought to also be that real deep assessment of "What's this person's character?" You can live with somebody who has immense outer beauty and be really miserable, but inner beauty. . . . That's going on in this story.

Boaz is really moved. He wants to let Ruth know he'd like to move forward, but he has to clear it with one other relative who may have a prior claim. So Ruth goes home, and then there's this really tender scene. I love this: "When Ruth came to her mother-in-law, Naomi asked, 'How did it go, my daughter?' Then she told her everything" (Ruth 3:16).

It's that last word, "everything," that makes me wonder how

the conversation went. Sometimes I can meet with a friend—even a good friend—and afterward, when my wife asks me, "What's going on with Rick? How's Sheri? How are the kids?" I realize I don't know the answer to any of those questions, and Nancy wonders what we talked about the whole time. (Not much, apparently.) But in this story, there is no such detail deficit: "Tell me everything! What were you wearing? What was he wearing? What did you say? What did he say? Did he kiss you? Is he a good kisser? Were you excited? Was he excited?" It's a beautiful moment in a beautiful story. It is one more tiny mark of Ruth's love for Naomi that she wanted her mother-in-law to feel fully informed. Sharing details was a way of sharing her heart. She "told her everything."

Then Naomi says to Ruth, "Wait, my daughter, until you find out what happens. For the man will not rest until the matter is settled today" (Ruth 3:18). The matter *is* settled, Boaz and Ruth are married, and they have a son. Naomi becomes like a second mother to that boy. They all live happily ever after.

Sometimes people become so obsessed with vocational open doors that they become blind to relational open doors. I talked to a busy, successful-in-his-career middle-aged man once who said he really wanted to get married. "Any possibilities on the horizon?" I asked. "Well, there was a woman who had indicated she was interested," he said. He asked her to contact his administrative assistant to set up a date. Oops.

Every heart comes with a door. Having the door of someone's heart open to you is one of the great gifts of life. To respond well requires time, energy, vulnerability, and discernment.

The best way to find hearts with open doors is simply to practice love. At the church where I serve, a group of senior citizens decided to get involved at a high school that serves many low-income students often from high-risk neighborhoods in San Francisco. They have a prayer team, a teacher-support team, a resource-development team, a "lunch ladies" hospitality team, and a tutoring team that they proudly say consists of old, gray-haired guys. (I'm not surprised. Some of the godliest people I know are old, gray-haired guys.)

One of them is Grant Smith, eighty-two. He goes to the local high school every week to tutor teenage students. One week he didn't show up, and one of his students said, "Hey, where's my homeboy?" An open door can make a suburban eighty-two-year-old retired pilot somebody's homeboy.

Love opens doors. One of the greatest examples I've seen of this is Louie Zamperini, who ran in the Olympics and survived months on a raft in the Pacific and then years of prison camp torture during World War II. After surviving all that, his life was nearly ruined by his anger and pain and alcoholism, until he surrendered his broken story to be part of God's larger one. Our whole church read his story in *Unbroken* a few years ago, and we invited Louie to be interviewed one weekend. His interest in and zest for connecting with every single person he could was astounding.

He talked about the importance of praying for people. When he returned from the war, he was at a golf club in

Hollywood when someone told him Oliver Hardy (of Laurel and Hardy) wanted to meet him in the locker room. When Louie got there, Oliver rushed out of the shower, hugged him soaking wet, began to cry, and said, "When you were a POW, I prayed for you every single day."

When people approached Louie, he would often pray for them on the spot. "Anybody can pray for somebody," he said. His life was energized because he didn't regard it as *his* life; every moment was an opportunity to connect with someone, to learn from someone, to make someone smile. The weekend he came to our church, he had broken his leg one week earlier and his doctor would not let him fly, so his son drove him seven hours in a car with a broken leg.

He was ninety-five at the time.

The Way to Fix a Broken Story . . .

But wait! There's more.

One last little detail, one tiny little punch line. An epilogue that will surprise every Israelite who reads it.

A boy is born to Ruth and Boaz, and Naomi is like his second mother. They name him Obed, and Obed becomes the father of Jesse. The last words in the book read, "Jesse [was] the father of David" (Ruth 4:22). *King* David. The *hero* David. It turns out that Ruth—a Gentile, a Moabite, a *pagan*—is the great-grandmother of David. It's remarkable. It turns out that David, the greatest king of Israel, is not a pure-blooded Israelite. He's part Moabite.

Remember, the book starts, "In the days when the judges

ruled"—those violent, oppressive, idolatrous days. Nobody knew it, but those days were numbered. Nobody knew it, but a king was coming. Nobody could have guessed it, but it happened because a pagan Moabite Gentile widow loved her neighbor as herself. She did something unreasonable with her life. She walked through an open door.

That meant she stepped into the blessings of the Kingdom of God. She became such a hero that her neighbors hardly knew how to describe her: "Your daughter-in-law, who loves you and who is better to you than seven sons" (Ruth 4:15). In that patriarchal culture, for a daughter (-in-law!) to be better than just one son was remarkable; to be better than *seven* sons—seven being the perfect number—must have been a world record.

But wait! There's more. Ruth became a hero not just in her own time, but she would be remembered forever and ever and be written about. And not just in the Old Testament. Her story didn't end with the birth of her great-grandson David. In the New Testament, remember who is called the Son of David?

That would be Jesus.

I love this. Jesus himself is not a pure-blooded Israelite. Jesus has a little Moabite in him. Ruth's story becomes part of Jesus' story.

Anytime you step through the open door, your story and Jesus' story begin to get mixed up together, and you become part of the work of God in this world. The only way to fix a broken story is to embed it in a larger story that begins and ends well. As it was once said, so it is said again. . . .

But wait! There's more.

CHAPTER 4

COMMON MYTHS ABOUT DOORS

Quite a few years ago, Chicago Bears coach Mike Ditka got fired, and at his press conference his comment was, "As the Scriptures say, 'This, too, shall pass.'" I've lived in Chicago, and "da coach" is a beloved figure, but he is not known as a great Bible scholar. It turns out there is no place in the Bible that says, "This, too, shall pass." It sounds biblical, but it's not actually in the Bible. That happens quite a lot.

When I was in seminary, I got in an argument with my

wife's aunt. We were on vacation, and she was saying she loves the Bible verse that says, "God helps those who help themselves." I said, "That's not in the Bible. That's actually opposed to the whole idea of the Bible, which says God helps us; we *can't* help ourselves." She said, "Not only is it *in* the Bible, it's my favorite Bible verse."

I said, "I go to seminary. I'll bet you twenty dollars it's not in the Bible." She stayed up all night looking for that verse. She couldn't find it, because it was Benjamin Franklin who said it. It's not in the Bible. (Actually, it's attributed to Benjamin Franklin, but I'm not sure it was his idea. I'm not even sure it's right to bet on what's in the Bible, but it was the only time I made money out of going to seminary, so I was glad for that.)

There are a surprising number of statements people think are in the Bible but are not. Like "God will never give you more than you can handle." Have you ever heard that one? It's not in the Bible. The Bible says God will not allow someone to be *tempted* beyond what they can stand, but the Bible never says God will not allow you to be given more than you can handle. People are given more than they can handle all the time. It drives me crazy when people think that's in the Bible.

Or "Spare the rod and spoil the child." Not in the Bible. Or "God moves in a mysterious way." It's in an old song, but it's not in the Bible. Steven Bouma-Prediger, professor of religion at Hope College, says that in his Bible class he will sometimes quote a Bible verse from 2 Hesitations 4:3. These are students in a Bible class at a Dutch Reformed college, and some of them don't even know there is no such verse and no such book in the Bible.

Another professor, Rabbi Rami Shapiro at Middle Tennessee State University, said he once had to persuade a student that the saying "That dog won't hunt" is not actually a verse in Proverbs. You know, "Verily I say unto you, that dog won't hunt." It sounds kind of like what the Bible would say, but it's not in the Bible.[1]

I bring this up because there's another statement a lot of people think is in the Bible but isn't: "When God closes a door, he opens a window."

The Bible never actually says that. Mother Superior from *The Sound of Music* says that, but the Bible doesn't. (There are a thousand variations on this phrase, by the way. My favorite is "When God closes a door, Julie Andrews opens a window.")

What the Bible actually says is "What he opens no one can shut, and what he shuts no one can open" (Revelation 3:7).

Far be it from me to criticize Mother Superior. (She's already got a hard title to live up to. Couldn't she just be Mother Pretty Darn Good?) But I think maybe part of why we like the "he opens a window" version is it allows us a chance to sneak back in to where we really wanted to go all along. The actual Bible version cuts down our options considerably. The first closed door in the Bible came after the Fall, when God evicted Adam and Eve from Eden and "placed on the east side of the Garden of Eden cherubim and a flaming sword flashing back and forth to guard the way" (Genesis 3:24). There's nothing in the passage about God also opening a window so Adam and Eve could sneak past the cherubim. The whole idea of God closing a door runs along the lines of "Don't go there." There's a reason we still pray, "Forgive us our trespasses." In fact, we'll see in a later chapter that closed doors can be just as much a gift as open doors.

But the frustration of the closed door didn't enter the picture until sin and the Fall; it will end when all things are redeemed. Opening doors for his creatures is what God loves to do. A basketball team often has a point guard who loves to make assists so that other players can know the glory of making a basket; it also needs a Big Man who loves to block opponents' shots. God is more like a point guard than a shot blocker. The doors God opens are like this: "unlimited chances to do something worthwhile; grand openings into new and unknown adventures of significant living; heretofore unimagined chances to do good, to make our lives count for eternity."[2]

But precisely because doors are about the future, and are about possibilities, and intersect deeply with our desires, and involve the mysterious ways in which God interacts with the world, our ideas about divine doors can be full of misconception and superstition. Sometimes we're just doing thinly spiritualized wish fulfillment: "If God wants me to go to this school that I really want to go to anyway, God will make the sun rise in the east tomorrow as a sign." Sometimes we appeal to Providence in an attempt to deny reality: "You can't break up with me; God already told me you're the one." Sometimes we cite open doors to justify self-indulgence: "God has made this giant, expensive mansion available to us so that we have a nice place to host church parties and traveling missionaries."

In the Bible, there is a world of difference between faith in a supernatural God on the one hand and trying to use magic or superstition on the other. The problem with superstition is not just that it's ignorant. It's an attempt to use some power or force without placing oneself in obedience to a Being who is concerned with justice and love.

When I try to use God the way someone uses a Ouija board or a Magic 8 Ball or a horoscope, I violate the nature of the divine-human relationship. I make me the master and God my genie in a bottle. I make getting the right outcome my idol. And I move away from the spiritual growth that is God's deepest desire for me; God's primary will for me is the person I become and not the circumstances I inhabit.

The children's show *Sesame Street* used to feature a segment called "One of These Things Is Not like the Other." Imagine that segment with three entities: faith, magic, and science. Many people in our day would say that faith and magic are like each other because they share a belief in the supernatural, whereas science does not.

But in a deeper way, magic and science belong together. People who believe that magic or science contains the deepest truths about existence hold that our biggest problems are "out there." Both science and magic offer power we use to remold our outer world to our satisfaction. Faith tells us that what most needs to be transformed is not our outer world but our inner selves. Faith is not about me getting what I want in my outer world; it's about God getting what he wants in my inner world.

How do I make doors a part of a larger faith journey and not an exercise in superstition? Let's look at some common myths about God and doors and the truth that lies behind them.

"God Is Not Involved in My Little Life"

One of the most crippling myths about God is that he is like some human CEO, so busy running a vast enterprise that the activities of someone as small and insignificant as me must not be the object of his attention. In this myth's thinking, I believe there are spiritual movers and shakers out there who may have great adventures with divine doors, but I shouldn't expect that for myself. I am either not spiritual enough or not significant enough.

In the Old Testament an official named Zerubbabel was trying to get the Temple rebuilt after years of exile and neglect. He was able to manage only a meager start, which was quickly overwhelmed by opposition from without and depression from within. He felt discouraged and like a failure. But through the prophet Zechariah came myth-shattering words: "Do not despise these small beginnings, for the LORD rejoices to see the work begin" (Zechariah 4:10, NLT).

A boy goes to hear a talk given by a great teacher. There is nothing special about this boy humanly speaking. He carries with him an ordinary lunch of five ordinary loaves and two ordinary fish packed by one ordinary mother. No one in that crowd looked less significant than him. And yet when the disciples were looking for food that could be shared, a thought shot through that boy's mind. He could share what he brought. He could give what he had. His small gift, in the hands of the Savior, became multiplied beyond his imaginings. For two thousand years that story has been celebrated.

A widow passes by the treasury box at the Temple. She places in the box two small coins, all that she has. She knows it will be the smallest gift given, that humanly speaking it can make no difference, that from her perspective it is almost foolhardy. She could not know that one man was watching her, that he would say she actually gave more than anyone else. She could not know that her story would inspire millions of people to sacrificially give billions of dollars over the centuries.

Do not despise the day of small things. For we do not know what is small in God's eyes. Spiritual size is not measured in the same way that physical size is. What unit shall we use to measure love? And yet love is real, more real than anything else. When Jesus said that the widow gave *more*, it wasn't just a pretty saying; it was a spiritually accurate measurement. We just don't have that yardstick yet.

No project is so great that it doesn't need God. No project is so small that it doesn't interest God.

One of the finest leaders and people I've ever known is a man named Steve Hayner. He is a person of great brilliance and competence, with a PhD from St. Andrews and a combination of emotional intelligence and organizational savvy that's off the charts. His early training was shaped by a remarkable woman named Mrs. Goddard, who had no "credentials" but had a genius for not despising small things. Steve was assigned to send out thank-you notes to people who had volunteered at the church. Mrs. Goddard told him, "You can't send thank-you notes out like that; the stamps are too ugly. You need to get stamps that will give the envelopes beauty and make the recipients delighted." He could have resented having to run such a menial errand. But instead he recognized an open door, an invitation to go the extra mile to thank people in the smallest of ways.

So Steve Hayner, St. Andrews PhD, went to the post office to get prettier stamps. And he never forgot that story, which has inspired thousands of others to put care into the tiniest acts. He went on to serve as CEO of a multinational organization called InterVarsity Christian Fellowship and later to be president of a great academic institution.

A few months ago, he was diagnosed with a very serious form of cancer. His world, which had grown so large, suddenly shrank back down to a small size—marshaling enough energy to receive treatment, being able to pray, saying thank-you. On his birthday, he wrote amazing words about how he was no longer able to "seize the day," but he could still seek to welcome the day.

When we are born, our world is very small. As we grow, it may become quite large. If we live long enough and grow old enough, it will become small again. If we do not learn to find God in our small worlds, we will never find God at all.

Do not despise the day of small things. Another one of those Bible verses that is hard to find is "'I love grandiosity,' saith the Lord." Mother Teresa used to advise, "Don't try to do great things for God. Do small things with great love."

Do not despise the day of small things, for of such is the Kingdom of God. A small thing is like a mustard seed, which in the Kingdom will be great indeed but looks small and insignificant to human eyes. It is like yeast, which eventually will permeate and transform everything but to us appears the smallest of ingredients. Babies and mangers appear small and insignificant—but that is how God comes to us.

Jesus mostly did small things. He talked with obscure individuals—a Samaritan woman at the well, a disgraced prostitute, a tax collector. He hung out with children so unimportant that his disciples tried to shoo them away. His final miracle before his trial and crucifixion was to replace a sliced-off ear.

We have no idea what is big or small in God's eyes. But for sure, I will never go through a "big" door if I do not humble myself to the task of discerning and entering all the small ones.

Do not despise the day of small things. For that, too, is the day the Lord has made. And that is where we find him.

"If I Can't Tell Which Door to Choose, Either God Is Doing Something Wrong or I Am"

I have learned this the hard way. Rarely when I have faced one of the "big door" decisions has the choice been simple for me. When I was trying to choose a vocation, I can remember praying for hours, being frustrated to the point of tears. "God, just tell me what to do, and I'll do it. I don't even care what it is. I just want to know."

Crickets.

I did not realize for many years that what I was looking for wasn't so much "God's will for my life." What I was really looking for was a way to be relieved of the anxiety that comes with taking responsibility for making a difficult decision.

God is a door opener, but he is not a celestial enabler. He doesn't even need the twelve steps—who would he turn his will over to?

This is foundational for understanding the notion of open doors correctly: God's primary will for you is the person you become.

The apostle Paul says that God "chose us in [Christ] before the creation of the world to be holy and blameless in his sight" (Ephesians 1:4). In other words, God's basic will for your life is not what you do or where you live or whether you marry or how much you make; it's who you become. God's primary will for your life is that you become a person of excellent character, wholesome liveliness, and divine love. That's what words like *godly* and *holy* (which too often become religious clichés) point to.

As I mentioned in chapter 1, making decisions is an indispensable tool in the formation of excellent persons. Every parent knows this. Imagine a parent who always commands their child's life and decisions. (You may be thinking, *That sounds like my parents*, in which case you'll need to see a counselor.

You may be thinking, *That sounds like a great arrangement!* in which case your children will need to see a counselor.)

If a parent's desire is for their child to become a truly good person, they will often *insist* that the child make his or her own decisions. Persons of excellent will, judgment, and character get formed no other way.

This means that God's will for your life will often be "You decide." Sometimes you will ask heaven for direction, and God will say to you, "I don't care." That doesn't mean God doesn't care about *you*. It means that God cares more about your personhood and character than anything else—which is of course what we would expect from a truly loving God.

Sometimes God may have a specific assignment for someone—like Moses taking on Pharaoh—and God is perfectly competent to make this clear. And wisdom itself will help us know the right course in many door selections, as we will see in the next chapter.

But it was a tremendous help to my understanding of faith and prayer when I realized that a lack of guidance from heaven regarding which door to choose did not mean either God or I had failed. Very often it was just the opposite—God knew I would grow more from having to make a decision than I would if I got a memo from heaven that would prevent me from growing.

"If It's Really an Open Door, My Circumstances Will Be Easy"

According to this myth, if I choose the right door, I'll be able to tell because my life will get easier. Choosing the right spouse means marriage should be effortless. Every morning we should wake up with sweet breath and sweeter dispositions. Nothing about the other person should ever really bother us—not *really*. She should make me feel great about myself, and when she is away from me, she should be looking forward to serving me.

If we have children, they should love God; get good grades; be above average in looks, IQ, social skills, and athletic ability. They should navigate puberty without acne or emotional turbulence, get into a college that will make us proud, and marry someone who will enhance our family's status. They should be completely and strongly independent while believing what we believe and doing what we approve.

If I've chosen the right vocational door, my job should bring me passion and fulfillment each day. My performance reviews should be straight As; I should be my boss's favorite employee, while the people who report to me regularly write me notes asking how they can make me more successful. Coworkers who are difficult to get along with should quickly self-identify and transfer to some other organization, preferably in Alaska.

If I choose the right doors, my financial life should be stress free. Someone should make sure that my pension or IRA or 401(k) is invested in vehicles that carry no risk and double every three or four years. I should be able to acquire everything I want while still having a well-earned reputation for lavish generosity.

If "easy" is my criterion for door judging, then every time

I hit "hard," I will be filled with doubt about God, myself, and my choice. But an open door does not promise an easy life.

In fact, when God calls people to go through open doors, what generally happens is life gets much harder. Abraham leaves home and faces uncertainty and danger. Moses has to confront Pharaoh and endure endless whining from his own people. Elijah runs away from a power-crazed queen. Esther has to risk her life to prevent genocide. The entire book of Nehemiah is arranged around resistance to Nehemiah's work that is both external and internal.

Paul wrote to the church in Corinth that "a wide door for effective work has opened to me, and there are many adversaries" (1 Corinthians 16:9, NRSV). Not just a door—a *wide* door. You could drive a truck through it. But Paul took the presence of resistance and opposition as a confirmation that this was the door God had opened for him.

Trouble avoidance is tempting but not ennobling. Spiritual maturity is being able to face troubles without being troubled. At the end of our lives, it's the troubles we faced for the sake of a greater cause that will have the greatest meaning.

David Garrow writes how Martin Luther King Jr. suffered during the Montgomery bus boycott. A low point came when he began to get hateful racist threats to not only kill him but bomb his home and destroy his family. At midnight one night, frightened and alone, he cried out to God that he was too weak to carry on. "And it seemed at that moment that I could hear an inner voice saying to me, 'Martin Luther, stand up for righteousness. Stand up for justice. Stand up for truth. And lo I will be with you, even until the end of the world.'"

Garrow adds, "It was the most important night of his life, the one he always would think back to in future years when the pressures again seemed to be too great."[3]

Jesus did not say, "My assignment will be easy." Rather, he said, "You will be handed over to be persecuted and put to death, and you will be hated by all nations because of me" (Matthew 24:9).

He did not say, "The world will be easy." Rather, "In this world you will have trouble" (John 16:33).

Jesus used the word *easy* only once. But it wasn't about our circumstances. The same Jesus who said, "I am the door" (John 10:7, KJV) also said, "My yoke is easy" (Matthew 11:30).

He did not say, "I'll give you an easy life." He said, "I'll give you an easy *yoke*." Taking on a rabbi's yoke was a metaphor for taking on his way of life. Jesus said that taking his yoke—arranging our lives to be constantly receiving power and transforming grace from the Father—would lead to a new internal experience of peace and well-being with God. In other words, easy doesn't come from the outside. It comes from the inside. "Easy" doesn't describe my problems. It describes the strength from beyond myself with which I can carry my problems.

Jesus' offer is ease of spirit on the inside, the presence of peace and joy in the midst of difficult circumstances. If I aim at easy on the inside, I can withstand hard on the outside. If I aim at easy on the outside, I will get ease neither outside nor inside.

"Open Doors Are about Glamorous Spiritual Success for Spiritual Giants"

Often we confuse open doors with spiritualized stories of getting what we think will make us happiest. However, open doors are mostly small, quiet invitations to do something humble for God and with God in a surprising moment.

Open doors to serve.

Open doors to give.

Open doors to repent.

Open doors to be honest.

If you ever think your life is too small or your work too unglamorous to warrant door-opening attention from God, you might want to read about the Rechabites. They were an obscure clan that perhaps shouldn't ever have made it into the Bible—it's thought that originally they had not been part of Israel, had not been at Sinai, and had not known the Torah. But they were told by Jonadab son of Rechab that God had opened a door for them to play a special role for him. However, it was a role no one ever volunteered for— they were not to drink wine, not to plant vines, not to sow seeds, not to build houses, not to settle down. *That's great,* they apparently thought. *We're excellent at* not *doing things.*

For generations they were faithful to those commands. It was an unglamorous calling—they lived as nomads, as though farming had never been discovered. No one thought of them as important leaders. They were the Middle Eastern equivalent of Amish hillbillies.

But centuries later, when Israel was on the brink of exile, it was the Rechabites that God used as a little picture of excellence in obedience. As a piece of prophetic performance art, Jeremiah invited the Rechabites to come to the house of the Lord. When they got there, he let them know they were just in time for cocktails. But they explained they were still teetotalers because of the ancient command. God told Jeremiah to tell all Israel to learn a lesson from these humble nomads that faithfulness to even humble tasks is prized in God's eyes. The Rechabite family—outsider, backward, unsophisticated Gentile goatherds—gave a lesson in inspiration and faithfulness to the people of God in their neediest moment. God commended the Rechabites and said they would always have a descendant serving him. In that day of tribal solidarity, it was a giant upgrade for the whole family.[4]

It's not the task we do that makes us great in God's eyes; it's the attitude in which we do it. God will open doors for people who have humble hearts, not inflated egos or outsized talents.

Often an open door is as simple as a second thought: Do the right thing, no matter how small. Do what any decent human being would do in this situation. Honor a commitment when it would be easier to let it slide. Sometimes going through an open door means just not being a jerk. If the door is not marked "glamorous," just settle for "obedient."

"There Is Always a Right Door for Every Decision"

No, there's not. If you really believe this, you'll never make it past breakfast.

When people wear spiritual blinders, they fail to look at all their options. Bishop J. Brian Bransfield says people often approach him with a dilemma; fret, "I just don't know what God wants me to do"; and look to him to act as a spokesman. He usually challenges them to broaden their perspective:

> Actually, there are eighteen things that God would be very happy if you chose. You're not cornered into becoming a priest or not. You're not cornered into marrying this woman or not. There are six billion people in the world. You're telling me that God looked at you and said, "There is only one thing you can do in your life, I know it and you have to guess it or else"? Could it be that you are putting *your* constraints on God?[5]

We are called to be perfect, not to be perfectionists. *Perfect* is unblemished excellence. *Perfectionism* is moral obsessive-compulsive disorder. The Bible says that God is perfect, not a perfectionist.

If there is only one right way to make a beetle, why did God make 300,000 species? If there is only one right way to make a person, one of us is off—and I bet I know which. Life is not a shell game where I constantly have to guess which cup the pea is under. To live that way is to bear the constant, crushing weight of guessing wrong. In Eden there was one wrong tree, but Adam and Eve were "free to eat" from every other tree (Genesis 2:16); they were not to try to guess which tree was the right one. God loves to give choices because choices develop our character.

"If I Want Something Badly Enough, God Has to Open a Door So I Can Get It"

Nope. He doesn't.

"God Can Never Force Me through a Door I Don't Like"

Pharaoh didn't want to let God's people go, but holding on to them turned out to be harder than he thought.

Saul didn't want to be king, but the crown came anyway.

Jeremiah tried to get God to give his office to someone else, but there were no takers.

Jonah tried to run away from Nineveh, but God is sneaky and has many vehicles at his disposal.

On the other hand, a prophet named Balaam wanted to travel to Moab, and God used his donkey not only to prevent his passage but also to confront Balaam with a "don't beat the donkey" message that anticipated PETA by a few thousand years.

The psalmist writes, "Do not be like the horse or the mule, which have no understanding but must be controlled by bit and bridle or they will not come to you" (Psalm 32:9).

The psalmist is distinguishing between two forms of guidance. One form is an appeal to reason and choice—the kind of guidance that is appropriate to mature persons. The other form—the "bit and bridle"—is the use of pressure and pain to force compliance. Usually if this happens in life, it takes the form of the law of consequences, and usually it means trouble. Don't wait for the pain of life to force you through a door that wisdom calls you to choose now.

"I don't have more time for my daughter," says the workaholic father. But his child, after years of neglect, runs away from home into a life of addiction and rebellion. He spends untold hours trying to track her down, and then with counselors and with programs. He had the time after all, but would not spend it wisely until he was forced.

"I don't have time to take better care of my body." But then comes a stroke or a heart attack or diabetes, and suddenly I find I have the time after all because my body is no longer able to do what I depended on it for.

"I don't need to work on my procrastination problem—at least not yet." But a series of unfinished projects and unfulfilled promises means flunking out of school or losing a job, and now I'm unable to pretend things will somehow all work out.

"I can handle my drinking/gambling/sexuality." But eventually a collapse comes. I lose my job, or lose my money, or lose my marriage. Pain and pressure force me to address what I have been refusing to acknowledge all along.

I think of a man I know who had a strong concern about the problem of educational inequality. But he found he was unable to let go of his desire to make a lot of money in order to give time to that cause. His financial obsessions led to alienation from his family, and ironically, his investments turned out badly. He had to declare bankruptcy. Eventually this led him to go into teaching at a school in an under-resourced area. His only regret is that it took him so long.

"If I Have Chosen the Wrong Door, I Have Missed 'God's Will for My Life' and Will Have to Settle for Second Best"

This is a form of what social scientists refer to as "counter-factual thinking," where people who don't like the outcome of one decision obsess over what might have happened in an alternative hypothetical scenario. The classic phrase is "If only . . . " "If only I'd taken that job/dated that person/chosen that school/made that investment instead of this one."

A businessperson comes to believe he should have been a pastor and lives with a chronic sense of guilt.

A woman believes she married the wrong man and fanta-sizes over an imaginary marriage to the man she now decides was God's Plan A.

We tend to do counterfactual thinking more often in a negative direction than a positive one. We think dispropor-tionately about those outcomes that disappointed us and not the ones that filled us with gratitude that we could have missed out on. And the wrong kind of counterfactual think-ing leads to paralysis, depression, self-pity, and stagnation. God is never calling us through that door.

Paul makes a helpful distinction for the church at Corinth.

He says there is a "godly sorrow [that] brings repentance" and a "worldly sorrow [that] brings death" (2 Corinthians 7:10). The right kind of sorrow over a wrong decision always creates *energy* rather than despair. It enables us to learn from past mistakes and grow into great wisdom. Godly sorrow is filled with hope.

Worldly sorrow is energy depleting. In worldly sorrow we look at our wrong choices as though the world—rather than God—is our only hope. We live in self-pity and regret. We obsess over how much better our lives might have been had we chosen Door #1.

God's will for my life is centered mainly in the person he wants me to become. He and I have all eternity to work on that, so I have never missed it—unless I reject it. All roads may not lead to God, but they all belong to him. God can use even the wrong road to bring us to the right place.[6]

Jesus did not say, "The Kingdom of God is at hand—regret and believe the Good News!" The difference between regret and repentance is the difference of an opened door to a new future.

God's doors, like his mercies, are new every morning.

Frederick Buechner writes, "The sad things that happened long ago will always remain part of who we are just as the glad and gracious things will too, but instead of being a burden of guilt, recrimination and regret that make us constantly stumble as we go, even the saddest things can become, once we have made peace with them, a source of wisdom and strength for the journey that still lies ahead."[7]

"God Is So Powerful and Omniscient That He Could Never Empathize with My Angst over Closed Doors"

One of the most famous pictures of a door in the history of art was painted over a century ago by an artist named William Holman Hunt. It shows the figure of a single man, standing outside the little home he wants to enter, knocking to be allowed in. We cannot tell if there is anyone inside or if the door will ever be opened.

It is inspired by a statement in Revelation 3. A few verses earlier in the same chapter we read of the "open door" God sets before the human race. A few verses later we read of the door to heaven that has been left standing open.

This time it is Jesus on the outside of the door: "Listen! I am standing at the door, knocking; if you hear my voice and open the door, I will come in to you and eat with you, and you with me" (Revelation 3:20, NRSV).

It is a humble thing to go to someone's home and stand outside knocking on the door, not knowing whether you will be allowed in. God has given to every human being the door to their own heart, and God himself will not force his way in.

That means no human being has ever faced the pain of rejection as much as God has. God is not just the one who opens doors; he is the one who stands knocking at closed doors.

God is the most rejected person in the history of the universe. If he is willing to stand at the door and knock, who am I to give up?

"Some Doors Are So Closed, Not Even God Can Do Anything about Them"

Actually, locked doors are kind of God's specialty.

I was in Cappadocia once and visited an astounding underground city that housed twenty thousand occupants in ancient times. They lived in caves that were constructed down to eight stories underground. I saw there an ancient, enormous round door made of stone. People would roll it in front of an entrance to seal it beyond opening. And in a new way I had an understanding of what got rolled away from Christ's tomb.

After that door got opened, all bets were off.

If God can open the heavy door of a sealed tomb, no circumstantial door is too closed to him. Consider what happened after the Resurrection:

> When it was evening . . . and the doors of the house where the disciples had met were locked . . . Jesus came and stood among them and said, "Peace be with you." . . .
>
> A week later his disciples were again in the house, and Thomas was with them. Although the doors were shut, Jesus came and stood among them and said, "Peace be with you." (John 20:19, 26, NRSV)

The doors of our lives are not closed to God. He has the power to enter into our circumstances and grace us with his presence. It's in the Bible. You could look it up.

CHAPTER 5

DOOR #1 OR DOOR #2?

How do I choose the right door? In Revelation 3:8 the church in Philadelphia is told, "See, I have placed before you an open door that no one can shut." But how do I know which door that is? And what if I go through the wrong door?

Should I date somebody? If I should, who should it be? How do I know if we should get married, if she is "the one"? What do I do if I know she's the one and God knows she's the one but she hasn't gotten the word yet? What school should

I go to? What should I choose as a major? What's the right career track for me to be on? What job should I take? Where should I live? Which house should I buy?

Does God want me to persevere in this difficult situation because I'm supposed to grow? Or does he want me to leave it because, after all, he wants me to be happy?

From ancient times on, human beings have wanted to consult supernaturally authoritative sources to know the future, to know which choice to make. They have read palms and tea leaves and stars and animal entrails. They have consulted oracles and tarot cards and Ouija boards. They have drawn straws and cast lots. In ancient Rome, augurs (from the Latin word for "diviners") studied bird flight to predict the future. It was called "taking the auspices," and even now we will speak of an "auspicious" day for action or suggest that something doesn't "augur" well for the outcome we want.

To this day such practices persist despite certain logical inconsistencies. People call the Psychic Friends hotline—if they're psychic friends, shouldn't they call *you*? If you're going to see a psychic, shouldn't appointments be unnecessary? I heard about one man who said he had almost had a psychic girlfriend, but she broke up with him before he met her.

The faith of Israel was quite intolerant of these practices—not just because they don't work but because of the critical difference between faith and magic. In fact, there's a weird and fascinating story about King Saul that helps us understand the difference.

Saul has rejected God's leadership of his life. He has

chosen the door of power, jealousy, deception, and ego. The Philistines are threatening war. Saul is desperate to know what to do, so he suddenly seeks "God's will for his life"— should he fight the Philistines or not?

But Saul doesn't really want "God's will." He doesn't want to repent, humble himself, confess his wrongdoings, or make restoration. He just wants the success of his own agenda. So heaven is silent. God cannot answer Saul's request in any way that would be truly helpful to Saul.

Saul can't get a response to his prayer, so he consults a medium in Endor and asks her to summon the dead prophet Samuel. (Necromancy—seeking to discern the future by consulting the dead—is one of the oldest forms of divination.)

Samuel appears and asks Saul rather testily what he wants. Saul answers, "I am in great distress, for the Philistines are warring against me, and God has turned away from me and answers me no more, either by prophets or by dreams; so I have summoned you to tell me what I should do" (1 Samuel 28:15, NRSV).

What is driving Saul (and often drives us) is given away in the first phrase: "I am in great distress." Making decisions is stressful. And sometimes I'm not looking for "God's will" so much as a guarantee of future outcomes that will take the responsibility of decision making off my shoulders. God *has to* tell me what to do for "I am in great distress."

Samuel does not give Saul the advice Saul is looking for. Instead Samuel repeats the moral and spiritual judgment that could have saved Saul but that Saul has already rejected.

There is a huge difference between faith, on the one hand, and magic or superstition on the other. In superstition, I seek to use some supernatural force to accomplish my own agenda. Martin Buber said, "Magic desires to obtain its effects without entering into relation, and practices its tricks in the void."[1] We are tempted to use superstition to be spared anxiety, or to avoid blame for our own wrongdoing, or to bail us out of trouble, or to seek inside information to get what we want. Magic gives us the illusion of knowledge when none really exists. Groucho Marx is supposed to have said, "If a black cat crosses your path, it signifies that the animal is going somewhere."

Superstition seeks to use the supernatural for my purposes; faith seeks to surrender to God's purposes. Faith teaches us that there is a Person behind the universe, and that Person responds to communication just as all persons do. Prayer is the primary way we communicate with God, and that's why prayer is so closely associated with seeking and discerning open doors.

But in the actual practice of our faith, superstition is as great a temptation for us as it was for Saul.

I once interviewed for a position at a church in Southern California. A woman at the church (let's call her Endora) told me she had prayed about this and received a "word from the Lord," which was that I would come work at this church but it would be in the future, not now. What she didn't mention to me was that her husband had applied for the same position, and if I got it, then he would lose it.

A man I know was once convinced that a woman he was obsessed with was God's choice for him. The ultimate confirming sign for him came when he heard a song that made him think of her on the radio and prayed that if she really was "the one" that God would make the same song play on another radio station, and the same song *did* play on another station. However, clearly he was wrong, because she married someone else. Plus, it was a song by Village People, and I don't think even heaven could use that.

Sometimes when I desperately want "God's will," what I *really* want isn't God's will at all. What I really want is what I want. Or it's to off-load the anxiety of decision making.

Princeton philosopher Walter Kaufmann coined the word *decidophobia*. He noticed that human beings are afraid of making decisions. We don't want the anxiety that goes along with the possibility of being wrong. Decisions wear us out.

I was at a restaurant once where the waiter responded to every choice we made by saying, "Brilliant" or "Perfect" or "Excellent decision." This happened so steadily through appetizers, entrées, and desserts that I finally asked him if he ever told anyone they made a lousy choice. He told us that the restaurant managers had discovered diners are afraid of choosing the wrong thing, so they actually print a list of "affirmation words" that the waitstaff are required to say in response to everyone's order. Even having to choose food makes us so vulnerable that restaurants turn waitstaff into therapists.

Choosing comes from the core of who we are. When we truly choose, we have no one to blame and nowhere to hide.

Choosing thrills us. Choosing scares us. Choosing is central to personhood. Poet Archibald MacLeish has said, "What is freedom? Freedom is the right to choose: the right to create for oneself the alternatives of choice. Without the possibility of choice a man is not a man but a member, an instrument, a thing."[2]

God wants us to learn to choose well. That may be why, when we look at the Bible, there is no chapter devoted to "How to know God's will for your life." Often when we are faced with a real-life choice, the Bible seems no more helpful than Yogi Berra's old dictum: "When you come to a fork in the road, take it." Paul doesn't write about "six steps to determine if he's the one" or "five ways to discern God's job for you."

What we do see are statements like this: "If any of you is lacking in wisdom, ask God, who gives to all generously and ungrudgingly, and it will be given you" (James 1:5, NRSV).

Or "This is my prayer: that your love may abound more and more in knowledge and depth of insight, so that you may be able to discern what is best" (Philippians 1:9-10).

God wants us to be excellent choosers.

Another philosopher has said, "Simple it's not, I'm afraid you will find, for a mind-maker-upper to make up his mind."[3] And God is growing mind-maker-uppers, not just order-carry-outers.

If I'm facing a choice and I want to find God's will for my life, I don't begin by asking which choice is God's will for my life. I need to begin by asking for wisdom.

Lady Wisdom Calls

Ever made a stupid decision? A Florida man died recently because he had entered a contest to see who could eat the most live cockroaches, and the winner would get a live python. He won, but he choked on the roaches. You have to wonder, what part of that whole venture seemed like a good idea to make somebody sign up?

If you've ever made a foolish decision of any kind—financially, vocationally, about your physical health or your spiritual health. If you've ever said something you've regretted. If you've ever made a foolish relational choice or romantic selection. If you've ever been less than insightful about time management or goal setting or parenting or television viewing. If you've ever made a decision that, with the benefit of hindsight, could be characterized by the word *dumb*, this chapter is for you.

We make decisions, and then the decisions we make make us: what I say, what I think, what I eat, what I read, where I go, who I'm with, what I do, how I work, when I rest. Add up 1,788,500 little decisions, and what you get is a life. We go through doors, and what we find on the other side is the person we've become.

The Bible has a word for people who choose doors well, and that word is *wise*. Not lucky. Not wealthy. Not successful. Wisdom in the Bible is not the same thing as having a really high IQ, nor is it restricted to people with advanced educational degrees. Wisdom in the Bible is the ability to make great decisions. Wisdom is the art of living well. The people of Israel loved wisdom so much they couldn't stop talking about it. They treasured it. They reflected on it. They celebrated it. They memorized wise sayings. They talked about it with their children.

They loved the story of Solomon, who when he became king was offered an invitation to ask God for any gift, and God would give it. Solomon asked, "Give your servant a discerning heart to govern your people and to distinguish between right and wrong. For who is able to govern this great people of yours?" (1 Kings 3:9). Solomon's first decision was to ask for the wisdom that would guide all his other decisions. And the text says God was delighted with this request.

In the book of Proverbs, closely associated with Solomon, we're told,

> Do you hear Lady Wisdom calling? Can you hear
> Madame Insight raising her voice? She has taken her
> stand at First and Main at the busiest intersection,
> right in the city square where the traffic is thickest.
> She shouts, "You! I'm talking to all of you! Everyone
> out here in the streets, listen! You idiots, learn good
> sense! You blockheads, shape up! Don't miss a word
> of this. I'm telling you how to live at your best. . . .
> I am Lady Wisdom. I live right next door to Sanity.
> Knowledge and Discretion live just down the street.
> The fear of God means hating evil, whose ways I
> hate with a passion." (Proverbs 8:1-6, 12-13, my
> paraphrase)

The biggest difference between people who flourish in life and those who don't is not money, health, talent, connections, or looks. It's wisdom—the ability to make good decisions.

The nation of Israel loved wisdom.

When I was growing up in the Midwest, if somebody said, "I really love this hot dog," it was considered very funny to respond, "If you love it so much, why don't you marry it?" It was considered funny where I grew up, but we had a low bar for what was funny. The Israelites loved wisdom so much they wanted to marry it, so they personified it. They talked about it as if it were a person. They talked about wisdom as if it were the most wonderful person ever in the world. In fact, they pictured wisdom as a woman. The reason the Bible pictures wisdom as a woman is that women tend to be wise.

In the ancient world, a lot of peoples had a lot of wisdom literature. In fact, parts of that literature made their way into the Bible. The people of Israel loved wisdom wherever they could find it, but they understood there is something more at stake with wisdom than just navigating life successfully in human terms. Proverbs says wisdom "has sent out her servants, and she calls from the highest point of the city, 'Let all who are simple come to my house!' To those who have no sense she says, 'Come, eat my food and drink the wine I have mixed. Leave your simple ways and you will live; walk in the way of insight'" (Proverbs 9:3-6).

In the ancient world, the highest point in the city was always where the temple would be located. This was true in

Jerusalem. In other words, Lady Wisdom is a poetic expression of the wisdom of God. Where wisdom is, somehow, God is.

So in the rest of this chapter, we'll look at some ways God's wisdom can lead us to—and help us through—the open doors we encounter.

Stop Waiting for a Spontaneous Outburst of Passion

A friend of mine named Andy Chan heads up the Office of Personal and Career Development at Wake Forest. Before that, he headed career placement at Stanford's Graduate School of Business, and the *New York Times* has said he is a "career-development guru." Andy says that one of the greatest stumbling blocks he has to warn young adults about is the illusion that there is some passion out there with their name on it, and if they could just discover their passion, every day of their working life would be filled with heart-thumping emotion and effortless, nonstop motivation. People read stories about successful leaders or artists or entrepreneurs and assume that once they chose their field, they woke up every morning supported by vast reservoirs of energy for their work. The pressure around this is analogous to the notion that there is one perfect soul mate out there in the world for you to marry, and if you don't find him or her, you're doomed to relational discontent.

No one's life is like that.

Thomas Edison used to say that genius is one percent inspiration and 99 percent perspiration. And life is much the same way. When I was a student at Fuller Theological Seminary, I had great admiration for its president, David Hubbard, who was also a prolific writer and scholar and speaker. Many years after I graduated, I heard him talk about how the most common misconception students had of his life was that it was filled with glamorous activities and inspiring moments. Most of what he did, Dr. Hubbard said, involved the consistent, plodding progress of one task following another. Write notes for a lecture. Chair a meeting with the faculty. Ask a potential donor to consider giving. All these tasks add up to a wonderful work. But they are not a series of moments designed to make you feel like you've just won the job lottery.

To believe in the significance of our contributions is an indispensable need of the soul. But to believe that choosing the right door will usher in a nonstop Niagara Falls of motivation is an illusion that will leave us mad at God and frustrated with ourselves. Don't wait for passion to lead you somewhere you're not. Start by bringing passion to the place where you are.

Practice on Small Doors

Often I don't think to ask for wisdom until I'm facing a big decision. But Paul writes, "Whenever we have an opportunity, let us work for the good of all" (Galatians 6:10, NRSV).

How often do we have an opportunity? Doors are everywhere:

- In a park a mom is watching her two preschool-aged children play. I could stop by for a moment and comment on what a gift those two children are.

- Early in our marriage Nancy and I were eating at a nicer restaurant than we were used to (it was a restaurant with no drive-thru lane). Someone who knew us saw us there and secretly paid for our meal. We have never forgotten that gift, and because that person did such a fun gesture, we have done the same thing many times for others. I have never done that and then thought to myself, *I regret spending money that way.*

- I have a free evening. Instead of automatically turning on the TV, I pause for a moment to pray and ask how I might spend the next few hours so that when I'm done, I feel good about the choice.

- Someone has his first day at the organization where I work. I remember my first day many years ago, how I had that "I feel like a kid in middle school and I'm not sure anyone likes me and this is not my desk" feeling. So I write an e-mail to welcome him to middle school and tell him I remember how it feels.

Choosing doors always involves a process: I recognize opportunity, identify options, evaluate, choose, and learn. If I wait until the giant decisions come, my ability to choose wisely will be underdeveloped. Making a life-altering decision is like driving the Indy 500 or playing before a packed house at Carnegie Hall: it's good to practice ahead of time. And opportunities for practice are everywhere.

Allow Time and Energy for Big-Door Decisions

One of the main reasons why "finding God's will for my life" is such a huge topic in our day is that we are overwhelmed by the choices we must make.

Barry Schwartz says his local grocery store offers 285 kinds of cookies and 175 brands of salad dressing. The menu at The Cheesecake Factory is longer than *War and Peace*. The beauty of blue jeans used to be their simplicity— they were blue, and they were jeans. Now you have to choose: boot cut, relaxed fit (what a gentle way of putting it), skinny cut, distressed (for pants that match your mood), acid washed, stonewashed, preworn, bell-bottom, straight cut, button fly, zipper fly, digital print, beltless, or unileg. (I made that last one up.)

We think having more choices means more freedom, and more freedom means better living. But having too many choices does not produce liberation; it produces paralysis. In one study, the more options people were offered for investing their pension money, the *less* likely they were to invest. Even though their companies offered to *match* the amount of money they would invest in retirement, people left the money on the table.[4]

We have turned our world into a smorgasbord of choice, and it's making us starve to death. We have become choiceaholics. And even the twelve steps can't help us, because it requires us to turn our will over to a Higher Power, and we don't have one more decision left in us.

Bible characters didn't face this. Isaac didn't have to ask

God whether Rebekah was "God's will for his life." He didn't have to decide which school to attend, and his career as an agrarian nomad was assigned at birth.

But there is wisdom for us from the ancient world. Open-door people tend to simplify their lives so they can save their finite supply of willpower for the decisions that matter most. In monastic communities people don't have to waste energy deciding what they are going to wear on casual Friday. John the Baptist, Johnny Cash, and Steve Jobs always knew what they would be wearing, so they could save their mental energy for more important issues.

It turns out that choosing drains us. It takes energy. So wise people shepherd their "choosing energy" well.

This is why wise people never make important decisions in a wrong emotional state. When Elijah found out Queen Jezebel was after him, he was ready to give up his prophet job and die. God gave him a giant time-out. Elijah took a nap, ate some food, took another nap, then had forty days of rest and prayer and recovery before he decided what his next steps would be. He was now ready to decide on the basis of his faith and not his fear. And his decision was very different at the end of forty days of rest than it would have been before.

I have seen people make terrible decisions when they were drained, tired, discouraged, or afraid that they would never have made otherwise. Never try to choose the right course of action in the wrong frame of mind.

Wisdom may well have you wait to make a big decision

until you're rested. An anxious mind and an exhausted body will lead to a terrible decision nine times out of ten. Paul says, "The peace of God, which transcends all [human] understanding, will guard your hearts and your minds in Christ Jesus" (Philippians 4:7). If I'm going to make a good decision, I need that peace, that encouragement of knowing I'm with God.

What's Your Problem?

Have you got a problem? Perhaps you're sitting quietly at home, at the breakfast table with your family, and your problem is sitting next to you. If you don't have a problem, call your church and they'll assign you one.

In a very important way, you will be defined by your problem. You'll be defined by your biggest problem. You can choose, if you want, to devote your life to the problem of "How can I be rich?" or "How can I be successful?" or "How can I be healthy?" or "How can I be secure?" Or you can devote yourself to a nobler problem.

Your identity is defined by the problem you embrace. Tell me what your problem is, and I'll tell you who you are.

People with small souls have small problems: how to make their lives safer or more convenient; how to put an irritating neighbor in his or her place; how to make wrinkles less visible; how to cope with cranky coworkers or lack of recognition. Small people are occupied by small problems.

People who live with largeness of soul are occupied by large problems. How to end extreme poverty; how to stop sex trafficking; how to help at-risk children receive a great education; how to bring beauty and art to a city.

You need a God-sized problem. If you don't have one, your current problem is you don't have a problem. Life is facing and solving problems. When God calls people, he calls them to face a problem. The standard word for the condition of being truly problem-free is *dead.*

Ichak Adizes writes, "Having fewer problems is not living. It's dying. Addressing and being able to solve bigger and bigger problems means that our strengths and capacities are improving. We need to emancipate ourselves from small problems to free the energy to deal with bigger problems."[5] Growth is not the ability to avoid problems. Growth is the ability to handle larger and more interesting problems.

One of the great questions to ask somebody is "What's your problem?" and you might want to do that right now. We ought to ask each other pretty regularly, "What's your problem?" by which I mean, "Do you have a problem worthy of your best energies, worthy of your life?"

What are you devoting yourself to trying to solve? How do you want the world to be different because you're in it? People who follow Jesus ask this question: "God, what problem in your world would you like to use me to address?" Followers of Jesus intentionally embrace problems.

A lot of times people want to know "What problem should I devote myself to?" It's part of wanting to know "What is God's will for my life?" This is the grain of truth that lies behind the illusion of spontaneous passion. I can't wait for an outburst of emotion that will motivate me forever. However, I can ask myself what need in the world produces a genuine sense of concern in my spirit.

Very often a sense of calling comes when people begin to pay attention to what moves their hearts. Often when somebody sees a problem in the world and gets all fired up, he or she says, "Somebody has to do something about that!" A lot of times, that's the beginning of the call.

There's a pattern in the Bible. Moses can't stand that the Israelites are under the yoke of oppression and slavery, and God says, "All right. You go tell Pharaoh, 'Let my people go.'" David can't stand hearing Goliath taunt God's people, and God says, "All right. You fight him." Nehemiah can't sleep because he hears the community of Jerusalem is in ruins, and God says, "All right. You rebuild the wall." Esther can't stand that God's people are going to be the victims of a genocidal maniac, and God says, "All right. You help deliver them." Paul can't stand that the Gentiles don't hear the gospel of Jesus, and God says, "All right. You go tell them."

What is breaking your heart? The walls, like the walls in Nehemiah's Jerusalem, are broken in this world all around us. Child hunger, the abortion of countless lives, human trafficking, lack of education, extreme poverty, millions of people who don't even know who Jesus is. There are so many broken walls.

Door #1 or Door #2? Your serious concern for one of the world's serious problems may tell you.

Pray the Lloyd's Prayer

Of course, when you begin to lay your problem out before God, things happen. An elderly man named Lloyd had a serious heart attack once, and the doctors told him he should have died, but he didn't. He was still alive. He started asking himself the question, "Why am I still here?"

That's another great question. "Why am I still here?" You might want to turn to someone you work with or live with today and ask them, "Why are you still here?" I ought to ask myself that question every day. "Why am I still here? Am I just here for me, really? Is the only reason I'm on this earth just to keep myself on this earth or to make my life more comfortable? Really? Is climbing a ladder what it's all about?"

We all know better, and the reason we know better is that the truth of the Kingdom of God, of spiritual reality, and of an eternal destiny in God's great universe is written on our hearts. Lloyd asked himself this question. He heard a speaker talking about using new technology to take a pre-recorded gospel message to preliterate people groups around the world. The speaker said it required a solar panel, but the panels cost forty dollars each, so it was really hard to make headway on it.

Lloyd found his heart pierced by the need people have for the gospel. Lloyd was in sales with Florsheim Shoes. He had never built a solar panel. He was not an engineer, but this broke his heart. He got all fired up about this. "Somebody ought to do something," he said, and he decided it was him, so he started praying over it. He got some engineer types and said, "You ought to design a cheaper solar panel for Jesus."

They did, and it ended up going into mass production. Over twenty thousand solar panels got produced because of Lloyd Swenson. They started to get used to spread the message of Jesus all around the world.

What's your problem? If you don't have a problem, you need a God-sized problem. Why are you still here? The reason may look dramatic. It may not. It doesn't need to be anything that feeds grandiosity, but we were made for the open door.

Ask Some Wise People to Help You

Everybody needs a door-selection committee.

Get wise counsel. If you want wisdom, don't try to obtain it all by yourself. Get around people whose character you trust, who have good judgment, who love you, and who care about your well-being. Tell them, "I have this decision. Speak into my life." Very often God speaks wisdom into us through somebody else.

Solomon, the icon of wisdom in the Old Testament, wrote Proverbs 12:15: "The way of fools seems right to them." Why? Because they're fools. That's part of what it means to be a fool, and there is a fool in all of us. There is a fool in me. There is a fool in you.

"The way of fools seems right to them, but the wise listen to advice." A coachable spirit is core to wisdom. We all need this.

I was working on this chapter when my wife called to let me know she just got out of court. She had let Baxter the Dog walk off the leash, and the Dog Police caught her and ticketed her. She went to court to fight this, even though she was completely guilty. The judge asked her, "Did you let the dog off the leash?" She said, "Yes, but it made him so happy." That was her primary argument—just dog satisfaction. (This defense got the fine cut in half. Go figure.)

Then she made a striking comment. "The court is filled with people who made bad decisions." I thought, *Well, yeah—you were one of them.* I didn't say that to her, which was a good decision, but I had that thought. Go to a courtroom any day of the week. Nobody is sitting in that courtroom because they had a wise, loving, trustworthy person courageously speaking truth into their life about the decision they made. The way of a fool seems right to the fool. And there is a fool inside every one of us.

Ironically, one of the greatest violators of this proverb, years later, was Solomon himself. Solomon, who had asked God for wisdom. Just a few chapters later we're told "[Solomon] had seven hundred wives of royal birth and three hundred concubines, and his wives led him astray" (1 Kings 11:3). No kidding. Here's a little piece of wisdom: don't marry a thousand women, and you're already ahead of the smartest guy who ever lived. Part of what Solomon's life tells us is the battle for wisdom is never over. You can have wisdom and make a lot of good decisions, but we all have a weakness. We all have a blind spot.

One of the best pieces of advice I ever got many years ago was to ask a few wise, trusted people in my life to be kind of a personal board of directors for me. I asked them if we could have a conversation about once a month for an extended period of time, an hour or two, about what matters most: my soul, my family, my marriage, the work I'm doing, my relationships, my emotional life, my finances.

The guy who told me about that is very near the end of his life now. He is one of the wisest people I've ever known. He has lived so well. If you have an important decision, right now think of one or two people you can go to. Ask them, "Could you speak wisdom into my life? Here's what I'm thinking. How does it sound to you?" Almost all train-wreck decisions people make (and we all make them) could be prevented just by asking one wise person to speak seriously into our lives and then listening.

The decisions we make are impacted by factors outside us far more than we know. In one study duplicated many times over, people given large buckets of popcorn ate on average 53 percent more popcorn than people given small buckets. It didn't matter what the movie was. Didn't even matter if the popcorn was stale. Give people more, and some mysterious part of the brain says, "I guess I'll eat more."

The environment around us influences the opportunities we recognize and the choices we will make. So make sure you ask the right people to help you.

In Acts 13, we're told that a community of believers gathered together and devoted considerable time to prayer, worship, and fasting. Out of that experience we're told that "the Holy Spirit said, 'Set apart for me Barnabas and Saul for the work to which I have called them'" (verse 2). How did they know the Spirit said this? What did his voice sound like? The text doesn't say. Perhaps it was a dramatic moment; perhaps it was a leading they only clearly recognized to have been the Spirit afterward. (Often we see God's direction better through the rearview mirror than through the windshield.) But what is clear is they received guidance from God *together*, as a community.

On our own we tend to miss doors. One error we make is called by Chip and Dan Heath "narrow framing": we miss the full range of options God has before us because of our restricted thinking. We ask things like "Should I end this relationship or not?" instead of "How might I make this relationship better?" Or "Should I buy that or not?" rather than "What's the best way I can use this money?"[6]

Very often the choice isn't Door #1 *or* Door #2. It's Door #14.

On our own we tend to suffer from confirmation bias. We seek out information that confirms what it is we already want rather than looking for the unvarnished truth. People watch cable channels that reinforce their political bias. We pretend we want the truth—"What do you think of my tattoo?" "Do you like my girlfriend?"—but what we really want is reassurance of the positions we've already staked out.

This dynamic was well known in biblical times. Isaiah talked about people "who say to the seers, 'Do not see'; and to the prophets, 'Do not prophesy to us what is right; speak to us smooth things, prophesy illusions'" (Isaiah 30:10, NRSV).

We need others to help us recognize our doors. But not just anyone can help. We need people with the wisdom to be discerning and the courage to be truthful.

Sometimes communities of faith can actually be *worse* at discernment. A man on a team at church makes a bad decision. When challenged by the team, his response is "But God *told* me to do this." Don't. God didn't. That was a stupid decision, and God is notoriously not stupid. It's in the Bible.

What's worse is attempting to manipulate other people by using spiritual language to claim divine authority for my own foolish will. When normal people change jobs, they usually give normal reasons: a promotion, more money, or a greater chance to contribute. There also might have been problems involved: conflict with a boss or a failure to work effectively. But in churches, when pastors say they are leaving, what usually gets said is "I got a call." *Calling* is too important a word to be abused by papering over conflict, incompetence, ambition, or unhealthy culture. Plus, such language often sends a message to congregations that pastors have access to a special "calling channel" about their vocational decisions that other people do not have.

God's calling usually involves very frank discussions about all these issues; it's not a way to avoid them. It's fascinating that in Acts 13 the church felt led by the Spirit to send out Paul and Barnabas. A few chapters later Paul and Barnabas had such a major conflict over a personnel issue that they split up ("the disagreement became so sharp that they parted company," Acts 15:39, NRSV). Luke's honesty is refreshing here. Many contemporary churches would say, "Barnabas just felt called to a new season of ministry, God bless him . . . "

Test, Experiment, and Learn Failure Tolerance

Does God ever have guidance for a particular decision? Of course.

Does he have guidance for every decision? Of course not.

I should be open to guidance—I should seek it and listen for it. But I shouldn't try to force it, and I'm not to take it as failure if I don't sense or receive it.

I have been in church ministry my whole life. I remember being told, "Don't become a pastor unless you can't possibly do anything else," a criterion that could create a less-than-competent pastoral community.

I didn't fall into that category. As best as I could discern, God was saying to me, "You choose." As best as I could discern, God understood I would grow if I had to make a decision in ways I never would if I got a postcard from heaven. That was the case for me at each church where I served. I never got a celestial e-mail. I had to choose.

Then a strange thing happened. I had been at my current church for a year or two. I faced a difficult weekend involving misbehavior by some staff members and other troubles. As I was driving to church, a terribly vivid thought entered my head: *Don't waste time asking if this is the right job for you.*

Don't waste time asking if someone else could do it better or if you could do something else better. You will grow in ways you otherwise wouldn't if you'll put your hand to the plow and keep working. Take your being at this church as my calling on your life.

I was not looking for guidance from heaven at that moment. I had already chosen to take this job more than a year earlier. But as best as I can tell, I think God was speaking to me. I think (as is often the case) his guidance was not so much about what he wanted to do *through* me as what he wanted to do *in* me.

I recognize that I am fallible about this. I recognize that calling is a communal rite and that it rests in the hand of the congregation I serve and not my own subjective understanding. But still. After all these years, I'm grateful for that sense of calling.

A call doesn't mean I can't fail. When our church was launching a new ministry, a staff member approached me and asked, "What if we fail? Does that mean that we didn't discern the will of God correctly? How do we know that we'll succeed?"

Discerning open doors is never the same as finding guaranteed success. God actually called many people to walk through doors that would lead to enormous difficulty and not external reward. Jeremiah was called the weeping prophet for a reason. John the Baptist lost his head. In Silicon Valley, where I work, venture capitalists will often make it a rule never to invest in someone who has not failed with serious amounts of money and time. Why? Because they know that people learn through failure, that where people do failure avoidance, they will never achieve the kind of courage and risk taking that lead to bold innovation. Why do we think that God is concerned with helping us live lives of failure avoidance?

In Acts 16, Paul is in prison in Philippi despite being called there in a vision. An earthquake shakes the jail and the prison doors are opened—but Paul does not walk through them! For him this is apparently not a particularly hard decision. Despite the door of his cell being wide open, he sees another, greater door opening to him. He has great clarity on the purpose of his life—to open spiritual doors for others. He can do that better in chains than as an escapee, as we see when his jailer comes to faith in Christ through Paul's testimony. Paul chooses the greater door, even when it looks like failure.

The Ultimate Door

Wisdom is wonderful. The nation of Israel loved wisdom. Ancient peoples loved wisdom. Wisdom makes for better friends, better character, better lives, better financial management, better workers, better communities, better citizens, better nations, better parents. But wise people still get cancer. Wise people still get betrayed. Wise people still die. Wisdom literature in the Bible recognizes the limits of wise human decisions. That's why in the Bible wisdom is something more than life management. Wisdom cries out from the highest place in the city, and then one day it came to the lowest place on earth.

There is an interesting wisdom theme in the life of Jesus. He said things so unusual that Mark says people asked, "Where did he get all his wisdom and authority?" Gradually, over time, these New Testament writers who had been raised to love wisdom, to revere wisdom, to cherish wisdom, realized that in Jesus something had happened. Paul marvels at the riches available in "Christ himself, in whom are hidden all the treasures of wisdom and knowledge" (Colossians 2:2-3, NRSV).

Paul writes this fabulous passage in Colossians that uses images describing wisdom back in the Old Testament, but here he's applying them all to Jesus. He says, "The Son is the image of the invisible God, the firstborn over all creation" (Colossians 1:15). See, that was wisdom. "In him all things were created . . . whether thrones or powers or rulers or authorities; all things have been created through him and for him. He is before all things"—now anybody reading that would recognize those are all the statements God made about the wisdom of God they had always loved so much—"and in him all things hold together" (verses 16-17).

"Christ, in whom are hidden all the treasures of wisdom and knowledge" (Colossians 2:2-3). God has done something amazing. Wisdom, which lives in the highest place, has come down to the lowest place. Wisdom seen in the Bible—wisdom seen now—is not just the ability to make good decisions. One day wisdom came into flesh, the Word (*logos*). All that stuff in the beginning of John's Gospel? That's all wisdom language. Wisdom came in the flesh, and Wisdom said strange things no one had ever said before.

People in Israel knew what their problem was: it was Rome. And they knew their options: Door #1 was to overthrow the Romans in hatred (the Zealots); Door #2 was to withdraw from the Romans in contempt (a group called the Essenes); Door #3 was to collaborate with the Romans in self-interest (the Sadducees). Jesus, who is Wisdom in human form, saw an alternative no one else recognized: sacrificial love and resurrection power. By choosing to embody this option, Jesus himself is the one who opened up the way to God for us.

And so he said, "I am the door: by me if any man enter in, he shall be saved, and shall go in and out, and find pasture" (John 10:9, KJV). The ultimate door is a Person.

Wisdom named the door less chosen: "Take up your cross and die to yourself, and then, if you die, you will live."

Wisdom loved, and Wisdom suffered on a cross, and Wisdom died, and Wisdom was raised to life again. Wisdom, thank God, is far more than common sense and practical advice and navigating life safely and well. Wisdom bets it all on God, dies on a cross, and gets resurrected on the third day. Wisdom is alive today and can walk with me through the doors I face. The writers of the New Testament realized that all they had loved and prized and cherished about wisdom they found in Jesus.

Jesus has a bride. This bride is called the *church*, and he's coming back for it.

If you love wisdom so much, why don't you marry it?

One day we will.

CHAPTER 6

HOW TO CROSS A THRESHOLD

A MAN NAMED SYLVESTER grew up in the Deep South during the Great Depression. He grew up to be a master at recognizing and entering open doors, a man of immense dignity and strength and courage. But my favorite door story about him is how he met his wife.

He met Barbara on a blind date. He had never seen her. She had never seen him. She had heard about him. He was an athletic young guy. (In fact, their son played in the major leagues for many years.) The doorbell rang, and Barbara went to the door. She was all fixed up. She opened the door, and there was a man looking back at her. But he looked nothing like she expected. He was a woefully out-of-shape man who obviously didn't take care of his body. He looked nothing like the athletic young man she'd heard described.

She stood there for a moment, surprised and confused, and then all of a sudden, another guy jumped out from behind him and said, "I'm Sylvester! You go with me!" She wondered what this was about. It turns out Sylvester had asked the other guy to come along because he had never seen Barbara before, and if Barbara turned out to be ugly, she would go out with the other guy. When he saw her, he was so excited, he wanted there to be no mistake. "No! No! No! I'm Sylvester! Not him!"

They were married for sixty years.

It's good to choose your doors carefully. But when you go—go.

I am not in charge of which doors will be presented to me through my life. I may not be able to force a closed door to open. I am not in charge of what's behind the door. But I am in charge of one dynamic: when a door is opened, I get to choose how I will respond. Sometimes it's what you do after the door opens that makes all the difference.

Often in life when we make a choice, we're tempted to obsess over the question of whether we chose the right door. Often this will happen most when it helps the least—when we're frustrated or depressed with the door we've chosen.

When I've done this, I've compared the best imagined aspects of Choice B with the most exaggerated difficulties of the choice I've made. I've thought about how friendly the people at Place B would have been, or how much better a fit Job B would have been, or how much better an education I'd have gotten at School B. (I didn't even have a Wife B, which is both understandable and extremely fortunate.)

What I don't recognize when I do this is that there is no script for how things would have gone with Plan B, just as there's no script for how things will go with Plan A. The biggest determinant of how things will go with Plan A is whether I throw myself into this new open-door season with great enthusiasm and prayer and hope and energy.

If I stew over what might have been, I rob myself of energy and spirit to see all the small doors God sets before me each day. I rob myself of precisely the spiritual assets I need to find life with God right here, right now.

In other words, often what matters most is not the decision I make but how I throw myself into executing it well. It's better to go through the wrong door with your best self than the best door with your wrong self. Sometimes the way in which I go through the door matters more than which door I actually go through.

Doris Kearns Goodwin writes that one of the reasons the American public loved Teddy Roosevelt so much was the irrepressible exuberance with which he embraced life. He never entered a door or a commitment halfheartedly. If he was in—whatever he was doing—he was all in. A contemporary of his remembers that with his great energy he even "danced just as you'd expect him to dance if you knew him. He hopped."[1]

Hopping is what children do. You can walk one step at a time, but hopping is something you do with your whole self. Hopping is what even adults do in moments of great joy, when they hit the lotto, or win the World Series, or pop the question and she says yes.

If you're going through an open door, don't limp across the threshold. Hop.

Often we fail to go through open doors in a wholehearted way because we experience what is sometimes called buyer's remorse. People are most likely to suffer from buyer's remorse in three conditions:

- I've put lots of effort into the decision (it cost considerable time, money, or energy).
- The decision was my responsibility (so I can't blame someone else).
- The decision carries high commitment (I can't move out of this house for a long time).

Key spiritual decisions often require high effort, high responsibility, and high commitment. That means they will often involve buyer's remorse.

We see this in spades in the Exodus. Israel is thrilled to go through God's open door of liberation from Egypt and slavery. But shortly after crossing the Red Sea, buyer's remorse kicks in:

We remember the fish we used to eat in Egypt for
nothing, the cucumbers, the melons, the leeks, the
onions, and the garlic; but now our strength is dried
up, and there is nothing at all but this manna to look
at. (Numbers 11:5-6, NRSV)

Meanwhile, Moses is having second thoughts about his
decision to go through the leadership door:

Moses said to the LORD, "Why have you treated your
servant so badly? Why have I not found favor in your
sight, that you lay the burden of all this people on me?
Did I conceive all this people? Did I give birth to them,
that you should say to me, 'Carry them in your bosom,
as a nurse carries a sucking child . . . '? Where am I
to get meat to give to all this people? For they come
weeping to me and say, 'Give us meat to eat!' I am not
able to carry all this people alone, for they are too heavy
for me. If this is the way you are going to treat me, put
me to death at once." (Numbers 11:11-15, NRSV)

Having second thoughts or buyer's remorse is an inevi-
table part of walking through open doors. It is not fatal. It
is not final.

Recognizing the angst of difficult decision making can
help you avoid one of the worst, overspiritualized traps
people fall into when faced with a daunting opportunity:
the "I just don't feel peace about it" excuse for capitulating

to fear or to laziness. In this scenario, we take the presence of internal anxiety as a supernatural rationale for avoiding taking on a challenge rather than seeing it for what it is—a simple sign of emotional immaturity.

"Why don't you end that relationship in which you're behaving like a needy, desperate, clinging vine with a person who's just not that into you?"

"Why don't you have an honest conversation with that person in your workplace/family/small group who is behaving badly and whom you are secretly judging and resenting?"

"Why don't you get out of your rut by taking this trip or that class or volunteering in those areas?"

"Well, I would, but I just don't have peace about it."

If "having peace about it" were the ultimate criterion for going through open doors, nobody in the Bible would have done anything God asked. The sequence in the Bible is usually not

- calling;
- deep feeling of peace about it;
- decision to obey;
- smooth sailing.

Instead, it's usually

- calling;
- abject terror;
- decision to obey;

- big problems;
- more terror;
- second thoughts;
- repeat several times;
- deeper faith.

Having second thoughts about going through a door is not unusual. It's not an automatic sign that I've made the wrong choice. It's not even a good predictor of the future. Israel fluctuated in how they felt about the decision to take the open door through the Red Sea. One moment they were terrified ("Defy Pharaoh? I don't think so!"). The next, elated ("The Red Sea has parted!"). Then the decision looked awful ("Manna again?"), then wonderful ("Get Daddy's shotgun—look at those quail!").

Never does the Bible command anyone, "If you're having difficulty in your marriage, try managing it by spending a large number of hours speculating on what would have happened if you had married someone else. Vividly contrast the hypothetical strengths of your fictional spouse with the high-definition flaws of your actual one."

There is a cure for buyer's remorse. There is a better way to go through the door—with all your heart.

Hop.

Discerning Wholeheartedness

I have never heard a football coach ask his team to go out on the field and give it 90 percent. You can't imagine a great leader standing before the team and saying, "Now go out and give it . . . most of what you've got."

I've never been to a wedding and heard a groom say to a bride, "With this ring I thee wed, and I promise to be devoted and faithful to you a pretty darn good chunk of the time." In fact, there's an old tradition that when a newly married couple crosses the threshold for the first time, the groom carries the bride. It's a picture of wholehearted trust and wholehearted commitment.

I've never seen a boss at a great organization interview an employee and say, "We expect you to give four-fifths of a good day's work." But sometimes people try to walk through high-challenge doors with low-level commitment. And the result is defeat. The greater the door, the greater the call for wholeheartedness.

You might be asking, "You mean there could be an expectation that I would voluntarily suffer loss, refrain from pleasure I could otherwise have, sacrifice my comfort, reduce my lifestyle, give up my time, confess my sin, be accountable to a community, or humble my pride?"

Yep.

The way to go through one of God's open doors is with all your heart. And "with all your heart" means that sacrifice is involved—choosing one thing means not choosing another.

A king in the Old Testament is described this way: "Amaziah was twenty-five years old when he became king, and he reigned in Jerusalem twenty-nine years. . . . He did what was right in the eyes of the LORD, but not wholeheartedly"

(2 Chronicles 25:1-2). Amaziah punched the clock, followed the rules, and checked the boxes, but his heart wasn't in it. He obeyed God—up to a point. He worked for reform—until it cost something. That's a miserable way to live.

Contrast that with this summary statement of David. God says, "I have found David son of Jesse, a man after my own heart; he will do everything I want him to do" (Acts 13:22). David is called a man after God's heart. This can be a little confusing when you get into his story, because he's guilty of adultery and murder and cover-up. He's a train wreck as a husband, and he's worse as a dad. But his heart belongs to God. His whole life is immersed in the presence and story of God. What lights him up is to serve God and love God, and when he messes up—and he does—he repents and wants to get right with God again.

The heart, in the ancient world, was the core of the person. It meant not just feelings, as we often think of the heart, but the center of one's being, particularly the will. So whole-hearted devotion reflects that which I choose to embrace with all my energies. In the words of the ancient hymn "Hokey Pokey," I put my whole self in.

When David led the return of the Ark to Israel, we're told that he danced before the Lord "with all his might." He put his whole self in. If we wonder what that dance looked like, the text tells us it involved "King David leaping and dancing before the LORD" (2 Samuel 6:14, 16). David danced like Teddy Roosevelt.

He hopped.

One of the ways you can tell what your heart is really committed to is to ask, "What are my dreams? What are the actions I freely initiate?" One hundred percent commitment is really a matter of "Where's my heart, really?"

When our kids were young, I remember one time when there was conflict between Nancy and me. It was about division of labor issues. "Who is doing the most work around the house?" Nancy felt like I was really doing too much around the house and I might burn out. Except for days ending in Y, when she felt like one of us might be slacking, and it wasn't her. As she was talking about her frustrations, my training as a counselor would kick in. I would listen. I would empathize. I would nod my head. I would sympathize. Here's what I was *not* doing: I was not saying, even in my spirit, "I'll do whatever it takes—serve, partner, argue, initiate—to get us to the place where we're not living in chronic, stuck frustration around this."

I was finessing my way out of having to honor a commitment. I was being nice and polite but avoiding actually doing what I'd said I'd do. I'm so grateful the person God had me marry will not let me get away with finessing commitment. I should say, *most* of the time I am grateful. My best self is always grateful for that.

Amaziah went through twenty-nine years of his life finessing his commitment to God. He did what was right, but his heart was someplace else.

I can tell what my heart is devoted to because I will find my emotions and worship revolving around it. David famously scandalized his wife by "dancing before the LORD with all his might" (2 Samuel 6:14). We all dance for something.

Have you recently crossed the threshold of an open door? How committed are you? Just as an EKG can measure the health of our physical heart, it's helpful to have an instrument that can measure the level of our wholeheartedness:

- Do I talk about this commitment to other people to create a kind of public accountability for my actions?
- Do I own the responsibility to grow? Do I read books and practice skills and meet with those farther down the road to help me develop?
- Do I complain about difficulties in a way that can subtly rationalize a halfhearted involvement?
- Do I deal with discouragements by talking with God and asking for strength to persevere?
- Do I recognize and celebrate even small steps in the right direction?
- The apostle Paul writes, "Never be lacking in zeal, but keep your spiritual fervor, serving the Lord" (Romans 12:11). "Zeal" is a great power; I am to track it and guard it. Am I honest about my "zeal" level these days? If my zeal is flagging, do I take steps of rest or renewal or play or discussion to renew it?

Jesus' Instructions on Going through a Door

We saw in chapter 4 that there are many statements people think are in the Bible that are not actually in the Bible. Here's another one that almost everybody thinks Jesus said: "Be in the world but not of the world."

Jesus never actually said that. The idea that we're to be "in but not of" the world has sometimes led Christians into the wrong kinds of separation, into a halfhearted being in the world.

Here's what Jesus did say:

> I have given them your word and the world has
> hated them, for they are not of the world any more
> than I am of the world. My prayer is not that you
> take them out of the world but that you protect
> them from the evil one. They are not of the world,
> even as I am not of it. Sanctify them by the truth;
> your word is truth. As you sent me into the world,
> I have sent them into the world. (John 17:14-18)

Where did Jesus send the disciples? Into the world.

That's a little vague, isn't it? If I were one of those early disciples, I think I'd prefer him to narrow it down a little bit. But Jesus seemed less concerned with which door his disciples would go through than how they would go through it.

"As you sent me into the world, I have sent them into the world." Jesus doesn't say, "Try to avoid the world. Don't let it contaminate you. Have as little to do with it as possible. Just hang out with Christian people in the church and try to stay away from people who use bad language and are bad people." He says being sent as an agent of God into your job, your neighborhood, your networks, your circumstances, and your situations is the reason you're on this planet. He says, "As the Father has sent me, I am sending you" (John 20:21).

This brings us to a dynamic about commitment that is observable in teams, in families, in workplaces, in churches, and in spiritual life generally. When somebody is deeply committed with their whole heart—not out of guilt, not out of obligation, not out of pressure but because they are convinced this is the cause that is supremely worthy of the devotion of their one and only life—they love to be challenged about that commitment. They love to be called to it, to be renewed in it, to be rechallenged for it, to have somebody say, "I'm going to set this bar really, really high."

When people are divided in their commitments, when they have compromised, when they are conflicted, they don't actually like to talk about their commitment. It makes them uncomfortable.

We see Jesus emphasizing *how* his disciples will go over *where* they should go earlier in the Gospel of Matthew. He sends them to go out in mission in pairs. (Interestingly, the text doesn't tell us who got paired with whom. That's what I'd want to know—but Jesus isn't preoccupied with the "who" question.) The text doesn't tell us specifically where they were supposed to go: "Whatever town or village you enter . . . " (10:11). Jesus pays little attention to the details I'd most want to know—where or with whom. But what he is interested in is *how* they will go.

He tells his followers how they are to be sent. He gives three pictures, each one using an animal, to describe how we are to go through the doors God sets before us. They are the three dimensions of wholehearted living needed to enter open doors well.

Sheep among Wolves

"I am sending you out like sheep among wolves" (Matthew 10:16). This is an unexpected metaphor. The sheep is not an inspiring animal.

There are animal nicknames for all kinds of sports teams. There are the Bears, Tigers, Lions, Diamondbacks, Wolverines, Badgers, Sharks—these are dangerous animals—Eagles, Hawks, Bulls, Panthers, Bengals, Raptors, Bobcats, Broncos, Grizzlies. I don't know of a single team—professional, college, or high school—called the Sheep. "The San Francisco Sheep" just doesn't inspire terror in anybody.

I can think of only one even slightly famous sheep. When I was a kid, there was a puppeteer named Shari Lewis. She had a little sheep puppet that for some inexplicable reason she named Lamb Chop. That's a terrible name to give a sheep. How do you make a lamb chop? You kill the sheep! Then you eat it. That's what a lamb chop is. But that's what she would call her little sheep puppet—Lamb Chop. That's just weird.

Jesus says, "I'm sending you out like sheep." He doesn't stop there. "I'm sending you out like sheep *among wolves.*" Question: How does a sheep go among wolves? Answer: Very carefully. Very *humbly.* The sheep doesn't go out and say, "Hey, wolves, I'm here to straighten you out! Hey, wolves, I'm going to get you to shape up!"

This assignment doesn't sound very glamorous. But when you think about it, it takes some courage for a sheep to be sent to the wolves.

To be sent as a sheep means I don't lead with how smart or strong or impressive I am.

But it's a funny thing. Doors get opened to sheep that would never be opened to wolves.

In Genesis, Jacob's whole life is grabbing and manipulating. Finally, in desperation, he is visited by God. He wrestles through the night and receives a blessing, but in the process we're told that he is wounded in his hip, and the wound does not heal.

He goes on to see his brother, Esau, and their long battle is over. When Esau sees Jacob, his heart melts. Why?

Maybe it's because, when Jacob comes walking toward him, Esau sees his weakness. Maybe Jacob is leading with his limp.

Doors get opened to sheep that would never be opened to wolves.

I heard researcher Brené Brown say that once when she went to speak on vulnerability, her talk was going to be interpreted for the hearing impaired. She asked what sign would be used for the word *vulnerable*. The interpreter had two options. Number one was two fingers bending in the other hand—it means "weak in the knees." "Weak" is not what she wanted. What was the other option?

Number two was the translator miming opening up her coat to reveal herself. Courageous, risky self-disclosure.

That's it. "Only," Brené said, "when I do the second, I feel the first."

If I go through the door with all my heart, I am vulnerable to disappointment and failure. I am vulnerable because I am not strong enough.

The paradox of Jesus is that vulnerability is stronger than invulnerability.

I ran into a man recently who had been my Sunday school teacher when I was about twelve. He chuckled with me about a time when I corrected his mispronunciation of a word. But it wasn't funny to me. I thought about my need to appear smart and how often that need has caused me to violate love. Somebody said that what the world needs is not more geniuses but more genius makers, people who enhance and don't diminish the gifts of those around them.

Sheep do that.

"I'm sending you out like sheep among wolves." "I'm sending you like Albert Schweitzer, who gives up his status as a brilliant theologian and world-class musician to serve the poorest of the poor on another continent, and it turns out to be the grandest door he ever walked through."

Usually when leaders want to fire up the troops, they will paint a vivid picture of how gloriously successful they're going to be. Listen to what Jesus tells his disciples the first time he sends them out. As you hear these words, imagine you're one of the disciples and you're in the huddle. A lot of times right before the game everybody on the team puts their hands into the huddle, and they get one last pep talk. Then they yell, "Go team!" and play the game. Here's Jesus' pep talk. These disciples are going out for their first game. And here's what Jesus says to fire them up:

> Be on your guard; you will be handed over to the local councils and be flogged in the synagogues. . . . But when they arrest you, do not worry about what to say. . . . Brother will betray brother to death, and a father his child; children will rebel against their parents and have them put to death. You will be hated by everyone because of me. (Matthew 10:17, 19, 21-22)

Go team!

Who talks that way? Why does Jesus do that? Because he wants his followers to know that following him is not a promise to be successful. It doesn't mean we're going to go out there and be covered with glory the way our world thinks of glory. Sheep are not heroic animals. Part of what Jesus is calling his friends to do is to die to the world's standards of heroism, success, and glory. "You're going to have to die to that. There's going to be resistance. There's going to be a cost. It's going to take a different kind of hero."

The church is always at its best when it goes into the world humbly, like a sheep among wolves. Ironically, a few centuries after Jesus, when the church did get some political and financial power, it lost much of its spiritual power. One Christ follower, John Chrysostom, was reflecting on this verse about being sent by Jesus like a sheep among wolves and how the concept was getting lost as the church gained power. He said, "Let us then be ashamed, who do the contrary, who set like wolves upon our enemies. For so long as we are sheep, we conquer. . . . But if we become wolves, we are worsted, for the help of our Shepherd departs from us: for he feeds not wolves, but sheep."[2]

Jesus said, "As the Father has sent me, I am sending you." When John the Baptist saw Jesus for the first time, he said, "Look, the Lamb of God, who takes away the sin of the world!" (John 1:29).

In Revelation we see a wonderful, fabulous picture. John says he has had a vision of Jesus, the Lion of Judah in all of his power. Then the metaphor shifts and John says he saw Jesus, the Lamb who was slain. The Lion of Judah came to earth and was the Lamb who was slain. "I am sending you out like sheep among wolves."

I keep a little note on my desk quoting wise words from a spiritual mentor: *Don't strive to advance yourself. Let God advance you. Serve others.*

That's how you go through open doors like a sheep.

As Wise as Serpents

Not just that. Then Jesus goes on to say, "Be wise as serpents" (Matthew 10:16, NRSV). "I want you to be as shrewd and clever as serpents." I love that Jesus included this one. So often people think of Jesus as this naive, well-intentioned dreamer who floated serenely above human difficulties and reality. He was not. Among other things, he was really serious about actually getting his work done.

This is part of what wholeheartedness looks like. You put your whole self in, including your mind and talents. Jesus wanted people who were not just devoted to him "spiritually" but who were wide awake and willing to face up to reality and actually thought about strategy and tactics and being effective. They would take failure seriously and try to learn from it and seek to get better. They would roll up their sleeves. As serious as any CEO would be about a corporation that's just trying to make money, they would be more serious about actually trying to extend the work of the Kingdom of God, because when something matters, you are careful about whose hands you put it into.

Somebody sent me additions to Murphy's Law that "anything that can go wrong will go wrong." One of them was "When you go into court, remember you are putting yourself in the hands of twelve people who weren't smart enough to get out of jury duty."

Jesus wants to put his movement into the hands of people who are as realistic and serious about actually prevailing, actually being effective (with God's help, which is the only way it happens)—to try it, to evaluate it, to learn, to be wise—as serpents were thought to be in that day. Be as crafty and clever and smart and shrewd as you can. That may not look impressive—I'm not sure all the disciples were as strategically brilliant as Paul. But God doesn't ask me to be Paul. He's already got Paul. He just asks me to be as "wise as serpents"

as I can be. I love that Jesus said this. A lot of people would
not expect it from him.

How do we know what doors God might open up for
us? Be wise as a serpent. Although open doors involve mystery and adventure, they generally do not come at random.
They call for a high degree of learning and awareness. In
particular, vocational expert Andy Chan notes that your calling or vocation in life will require you to master two areas
of knowledge: knowing yourself and knowing the world you
want to impact.[3]

We might visualize such knowledge like this:

I can either be high or low in my self-awareness, and high
or low in my awareness of the world around me that I want
to impact. If I am high in self-awareness but low in world
awareness, I'm a *hermit*. I'm tuned in to my own thoughts
and feelings but don't know how to connect them to help
God's world. If I'm highly aware of the world around me but
low in self-awareness, I'm a *chameleon*. I'm exquisitely tuned

self-awareness

	CHAMELEON	CHANGE AGENT
world-awareness	CLUELESS	HERMIT

in to the world around me, but I don't know about the gifts and values that God has designed for me to bring to it, so I just blend in. If I'm low in self-awareness and low in awareness of my world, I'm *clueless.*

But if I'm deeply aware of myself and deeply aware of the world around me, then I'm ready to be a *change agent.* That's being wise as a serpent.

SELF-AWARENESS

Who are you? Andy says that this question is the foundation of all vocational exploration and career development. By having a clear sense of your interests and strengths (those skills that you are good at and enjoy using most), aptitude, talents, personality, aspirations, and life experiences, you can begin to envision the type of work—and life—that would be appealing and meaningful to you. Perhaps you love learning, or you come alive when you are leading people or building a team. Maybe you are creative and artistic, and you love beauty. Or you might delight in bringing order to chaos, or in bringing healing to the hurting. Maybe you already have a highly accurate intuition of all this. However, likely you would benefit from working with wise, balanced, and unbiased mentors to clarify and confirm your unique wiring. By knowing yourself, you will develop a new set of valuable lenses to evaluate potential opportunities and to prioritize work that you could pursue and work that you probably shouldn't.

A crucial aspect of knowing yourself is being able to define where your self-identity resides. Often people's dreams and career interests are driven by what they think will please their parents, impress their friends, be acceptable to their spouse, or provide personal benefits like money, power, influence, or prestige. Some can name these attachments; others can't without an external perspective as well as reflective introspection. These attachments are often things that people might perceive as important to them but, upon close examination, really are not.

If I know what most motivates me, I will be able to live a life of sustained engagement. If I know my wounds and weaknesses, I will be able to grow and perhaps even conquer them. If I know the kind of people I best work with, I will be able to be part of a team and not just a solo act. So self-awareness means looking at my passions, my scars, and my partners.

Passion is that area of life that fires you up, what I talked about in the last chapter as your problem. It might be world hunger, or it may be neglected veterans, or maybe it's education. You see little kids growing up in underresourced school districts, and they're never going to have a chance to learn, and it just kills you. Or you see people with AIDS who have been not only marginalized but are stigmatized, left alone, and hopeless. Or unwed moms, or just the cause of evangelism and the gospel being proclaimed clearly. There will be something that fires up your passion. Your passion is what makes you hop.

An often overlooked area of self-knowledge is to be aware of your *scars*, where you've been hurt, because that will equip you to help other people. I talked to a man this weekend whose son has severe autism, and this dad has created a community for other parents in similar situations that's just breathtaking. From people who battle addictions, to folks who have been in prison, to folks who wrestle with emotional disorders, to those who are unemployed—just area after area. God never wastes a hurt.

Then there will be *partners*. Jesus never sent out his disciples in isolation. He called twelve of them, and then when he sent them out on a mini-mission, he sent them out two by two so they could go together. So in addition to your passions and strengths and scars, there will be people in your life who will affirm you, cheer you on, and participate in what you're doing.

This is all awareness of yourself. But you'll also need an awareness of that particular part of the world you want to impact.

WORLD AWARENESS

Andy says that often job seekers know very little about the careers they claim are of interest to them:

> In the past decade, frequently mentioned careers
> of interest include thoracic surgeon, forensic
> investigator and lawyer. This makes sense since
> popular television shows have included *Grey's
> Anatomy*, *CSI*, and *The Good Wife*. This is a good
> example of how people are heavily influenced by

what they watch and read and place into their
minds, bodies, hearts, and spirits. Honestly, most
don't have any idea about what these careers truly
entail, what's required to succeed, and if the work
aligns with their interests, values, strengths, personal
"wiring," and aspirations.[4]

Wise people become students of the world as well as
themselves. They research ministry opportunities and job
descriptions. They talk to people who are engaged in the
kind of work or volunteering that interests them. They gather
information about such possibilities all the time in conversa-
tions and reading and experiences. They run time-limited
experiments and monitor both the outcome and their own
responses. They reflect.

We are never too old for this.

A woman recently turned eighty years old, and she didn't
want gifts for herself. What kills her when she looks at the
world is that there are places where women, *millions* of
women, have to spend two or three hours every day walking
to a well to get potable water. It's such an area of deep need in
our world. So she told people, "Don't give me gifts; help me
fund a well." She has currently funded three wells in under-
resourced parts of the world and is working on a fourth.

Eighty years old, and she's still hopping.

The need doesn't have to be dramatic. Open doors are
everywhere. One of them is in the post office in San Pedro,
California. It is the world's greatest post office. Workers greet

you at the door, joke with you in line, and hold contests to see who can help the most. One other thing: they don't get paid. It's the world's only all-volunteer post office, and it has been for fifty years.

A volunteer named Marsha Hebert took early retirement and looked around for something to do. "I looked at the post office, and I thought, 'That's for me!' because you interface with the public, and I also say it staves away Alzheimer's, because you have to be thinking all the time."

Not only do the volunteers benefit the mail-using public, but all the money they generate goes to charity—hundreds of thousands of dollars every year.[5]

No door is so small or so ordinary that it cannot be one of God's open doors, as long as you're shrewd enough to see it. Even the door to the post office.

Be Innocent as Doves

There is one more dimension of wholehearted threshold crossing: "Be . . . as innocent as doves" (Matthew 10:16). Doves are for the bird world kind of what sheep are for the animal world. They are thought of as quite innocent creatures. The main thing Jesus sends into the world is not what we do; it's who we are. This, too, is a mark of wholeheartedness. What the world needs is not simply isolated outward deeds but transformed character from within. That's what Jesus wants to release in the world.

I have a friend who is a doctor. A couple of years ago he had a patient who came in for an exam, and he overlooked one of her symptoms. She found out a year later she had cancer. It could have been detected by him a year earlier, except he overlooked this particular symptom that, as it turns out, was caused by cancer. As you can imagine, when he found out, he was devastated.

He didn't check in with anyone. The first thing he did was to call her up, get into his car (this is a doctor, remember), drive to her house, sit with her and her husband on their porch, and say, "I am so sorry. I should have seen that. I didn't. I will do anything I can to help you. Will you forgive me?" Guess what the legal department did when they found out what he had done. He did not get a gold star. But a funny thing happened. He and this woman and her husband cried together. This doctor prayed for them. It's a really cool story.

There was a study on lawsuits recently. What kind of doctor is least likely to be sued? The correct answer surprised me. The kind of doctor who gets sued least often is a doctor who is likable. The particular specialty or field is irrelevant. A lot of times in our legalistic world we don't think this way. We forget about the nature of the human condition. But the number one determiner of who gets sued is not who is most or least brilliant. It's not whether there's genius; it's whether there's humanity, just simple humanity.

The words of this strange doctor who admitted he made a mistake spread quite a bit in his little part of the country and have inspired integrity in other folks. What's interesting is he didn't do it to avoid a lawsuit. He did it because he's a follower of Jesus. That's the kind of thing followers of Jesus do. There's not always a rule or a formula for this. But this is what it means to be sent and to go wholeheartedly.

Jesus says, "As the Father sent me, so I send you. I want you to go like a sheep among wolves. I want you to be as shrewd, canny, clever, and wise as a serpent, but I want you to be as innocent as a dove. I want you to allow God to work on your character, because the main thing you take into the world is not the stuff you do; it's who you are."

Better to go through the wrong door with the right heart than the right door with the wrong heart.

The Dance of the Open Door

When author and teacher Brennan Manning was ordained a priest, he was offered this blessing:

> May your expectations all be frustrated,
>   May all of your plans be thwarted,
>   May all of your desires be withered into nothingness,
>   That you may experience the powerlessness and
> poverty of a child and can sing and dance in the love
> of God the Father, Son and Holy Spirit.[6]

The doors available to us may often confuse us. We think our work or our accomplishments or our family have to turn out a certain way—they seldom do. But life, this blessing says, depends less on which doors you go through—your expectations, your plans, your desires—than on how you go through them.

When you go through an open door, go through it with all your heart, with the powerlessness and poverty of a child, singing and dancing in the love of God.

For the blessing Brennan received was the blessing of Jesus. Jesus himself went through what, to human eyes, looked like one strange door after another. His followers expected him to overthrow Rome, but those expectations were frustrated. He desired to be spared the Cross ("May this cup be taken from me"—Matthew 26:39), but his desire was denied. He taught his followers they must become like a child, and he himself entered so deeply into powerlessness that "taking the form of a slave . . . , he humbled himself and became obedient to the point of death—even death on a cross" (Philippians 2:7-8, NRSV).

After he was crucified, on the third day, Jesus went through the final open door, the one that led to the defeat of death and the triumph of hope, the door that led to Somewhere over the Rainbow and the Land That Time Forgot and Home. No one was there to witness that moment. None of the Gospel writers record precisely how he crossed the threshold, but I think I know how he did it. I don't think he trudged wearily. I don't think he limped out that door.

I think he hopped.

I think maybe he's hopping still.

CHAPTER 7

WHAT OPEN DOORS WILL TEACH YOU—ABOUT YOU

WE ALL SUFFER from a kind of personal blind spot.

In a group, if someone is operating off kilter; if everybody is singing but one person is singing off-key; if someone has an irritating mannerism; if someone talks too much; if someone is a name-dropper; if someone violates other people's personal space and gets too close; if somebody is emotionally needy and everybody cringes when they see that person coming because they know that person is going to suck the life out of them—if some person has a problem, who is the *last* person to know?

The person who has the problem.

The truth about you is you don't know the truth about you. Other people know. They talk about it—with each other.

When we lived in Chicago, I used to go to a restaurant every week for breakfast with a friend. He loved waffles, but the restaurant didn't serve them. Every week we'd have the same server; every week he'd ask if they had waffles; every week she said no—he had no clue how irritating his behavior was. He didn't even realize he was doing it.

One day she finally melted down: "Listen, Waffle Boy—we don't have waffles. We don't make waffles, we don't serve them, we don't put them on the menu. We didn't have waffles last week, we don't have them this week, and we won't have them next week. 'Hello—Clue Phone—it's for you.'"

The funny thing is I told that story at our church. Literally dozens of people started going to that restaurant and asking for waffles, and they finally put them on the menu. Which kind of dilutes the point of the story: the truth about you is you don't even know what the truth about you is.

Fyodor Dostoyevsky writes,

Every man has reminiscences which he would not tell to everyone, but only to his friends. He has other matters in his mind which he would not reveal even to his friends, but only to himself, and that in secret. But there are other things which a man is afraid to tell even to himself, and every decent man has a number of such things stored away in his mind.[1]

Self-awareness is essential to the offer of an open door. Responding to the open doors God sets before us is a matter of not only being aware of what's going on outside us but being aware of what's going on inside us. Choosing which door to enter involves not just reading my circumstances but reading myself. "By the grace given to me I say to everyone among you not to think of yourself more highly than you ought to think, but to think with sober judgment, each according to the measure of faith that God has assigned," Paul writes (Romans 12:3, NRSV).

In order to choose doors wisely, you must become the world's leading expert on you. Not in a self-absorbed way. There is a world of difference between self-awareness and self-preoccupation. You must become aware of how God wired you, of what your interests and values and aptitudes are. And you must become aware of those parts of yourself that you most wish to avoid. Discerning open-door opportunities around you requires awareness of the world that lies inside you. And lack of self-awareness is a crippling handicap that no amount of talent can overcome.

When God set an open door before the church at Philadelphia, he also offered them a few observations about themselves. "I know that you have little strength," he said (Revelation 3:8). That's probably not what they wanted to hear. We don't know in what sense they had little strength;

perhaps they were few in number, or lacked financial resources, or were low in status and education. This is a letter that circulated among seven churches, so not only did their church have to hear that God thought they had little strength, but six other churches had to hear it as well. They would have to accept this truth about themselves if they were to go through the open door. They would have to go through the door in God's strength, not theirs.

At the same time, "little strength" was not the only truth about them. They were also told, "Yet you have kept my word and have not denied my name" (Revelation 3:8). In addition to being little strengths, they were also word keepers and name honorers. There was an obedient heart and a persistent spirit about them that would serve them well. And God's offer of an open door came with the whole truth about them—both negative and positive.

In this chapter we'll explore the various ways that recognizing and going through open doors reveals and requires us to face the truth about ourselves.

What Are My Strengths and Weaknesses?

If I'm going to understand which doors God is likely to set before me, I'll have to have some sense of what my gifts and strengths and weaknesses and interests are. Paul goes directly from telling people to think of themselves with sober judgment to speaking about how important it is that people understand they have been given particular spiritual gifts—for teaching or exhorting or giving or leading and so on.

When I went to graduate school, I knew I was interested in psychology and what makes people behave the way they do. I chose a six-year program where I would get a PhD in clinical psychology as well as a divinity degree. I assumed I would probably spend a good deal of my career doing therapy with people.

And then I started doing therapy with people.

My very first client was a disaster. My teacher was Neil Warren, who would later become famous as the founder of eHarmony. Neil had been trained at the University of Chicago, where Carl Rogers famously taught nondirective, client-centered therapy. So we were instructed along those lines. In client-centered therapy, the therapist is to give no directives, offer no advice, not even ask any questions. We were to simply reframe the client's comments to communicate unconditional acceptance and positive regard.

We were also being tape-recorded so our supervisor could make sure we were on target.

A young woman stepped into the room I used as an office. She didn't want to be there, she said. Her husband had signed her up against her will. "What are we supposed to do?" she asked me.

I looked at the tape recorder.

"What I hear you saying is that you're not sure what comes next," I said.

"Yes. That's what I just said. What's the plan?" she asked again.

I looked at the tape recorder again.

"My sense is that you are feeling uncertain about exactly what the next step will be."

It went on like this for the next fifty minutes.

It was so painful to me that after we were done, I went to the school library and read the newspaper for an hour because I couldn't stand to tell anyone or think about how badly it had gone.

I did keep seeing that woman for the next several weeks. And I'd love to tell you that she blossomed. I'd love to tell you that today that woman is—Oprah Winfrey!

But she's not. She eventually dropped out altogether.

And I realized that if I had to spend the rest of my life in a small room duplicating that experience, I would prefer a life term in a Siberian prison. This was not a good sign.

It's not that I didn't value therapy, or the process of healing that takes place through helping. I do. I'm grateful for it in my own life. It's not even that I'm so terrible at it. Over time as I went through grad school, I actually had some clients who didn't drop out.

But I learned something early on that I'm still grateful for.

Marcus Buckingham notes that your strengths are not simply what you're good at, and your weaknesses are not simply what you're bad at. You will have some activities in your life that you might even be pretty effective at doing, but they drain you.

What do you call that? Something you've been blessed with lots of ability to do well but cursed

with no appetite for it. . . . You call that a *weakness*.
A weakness is any activity that leaves you feeling
weaker after you do it. It doesn't matter how good
you are at it or how much money you make doing
it, if doing it drains you of energy, you'd be crazy to
build your career around it.[2]

One of the biggest difficulties for me was the thought
that I was wasting all the money and years I had invested
in going to grad school. Economists sometimes speak of the
dangers of "sunk costs," the temptation to keep throwing
money into a losing venture because we can't stand to face
up to the loss.

But how much worse it would have been if I'd spent the
next forty years of my life going through wrong doors and
misspending my life sitting in little rooms doing bad therapy.
Better to acknowledge that I walked through a wrong door
than to spend the rest of my life in the wrong room.

The apostle Paul said, "We are what he has made us, created in Christ Jesus for good works, which God prepared
beforehand to be our way of life" (Ephesians 2:10, NRSV).
In other words, the same God who made you also made the
doors for you to go through and the tasks for you to do. As
a general rule he will give you not only the skill but also the
interest to do what he asks you to do over the long haul.

Rigorous self-awareness about your strengths and weaknesses and interests will be critical to learning about the doors
set before you.

What Is Driving Me?

Being honest about the doors I hope to go through will bring me face-to-face with the truth about my motivations and ambitions and grandiosity. I recently got a copy of a letter I wrote twenty-five years ago. I had read a book by Dallas Willard and wrote to tell him how much it meant to me. In turn he invited me to come meet with him, and that opened a door to a friendship that changed my life.

After Dallas's death in the spring of 2013, his daughter sent me a copy of that letter. Dallas had kept it all these years. I have saved it in that book I loved. I treasure that note. Except for three letters. I signed it "John Ortberg, PhD."

Really? I had to impress Dallas with my credentials?

Meeting Dallas opened a door for learning and growth that I treasure. But it was embarrassing to read how impure my motives were, how even in that first contact I was doing impression management.

However, if I wait to go through a door until my motives are pure, I will never go through any doors. But if I want to go with God, I'll have to be willing to look at truths about me I'd rather not see. We see this in an amazing story in Matthew 20:

> Jesus was going up to Jerusalem. On the way, he
> took the Twelve aside and said to them, "We are
> going up to Jerusalem, and the Son of Man will be
> delivered over to the chief priests and the teachers of
> the law. They will condemn him to death and will

hand him over to the Gentiles to be mocked and flogged and crucified. On the third day he will be raised to life!" Then the mother of Zebedee's sons [James and John] came to Jesus with her sons and, kneeling down, asked a favor of him. "What is it you want?" he asked. She said, "Grant that one of these two sons of mine may sit at your right and the other at your left in your kingdom." (verses 17-21)

This is an amazing moment. Jesus tells his disciples he's on his way to die. Matthew writes, "*Then* the mother of Zebedee's sons came. . . . " In other words, immediately after Jesus says he has to be betrayed, condemned, mocked, flogged, and crucified, she says, "Before that happens, can I get in a quick ask?" *This is good timing. I can get this in just under the wire.* "Jesus, would you do me a solid? You know my boys here, Jimmy and Johnny. Before you're humiliated and martyred in the ultimate act of self-emptying, sacrificial love, could I get my boys a promotion? Could I get them an upgrade? I know you have twelve disciples and all, but could you make sure my boys are disciple number one and disciple number two?"

This pattern of Jesus explaining his call to suffering and the disciples angling for greatness occurs three times in Matthew. Dale Bruner says, "The gospel wants disciples to know their congenital obtuseness."[3]

The boys don't have to ask Jesus themselves, because Mom is going to do that for them. They can just stand there and look sheepish and modest as if, of course, they wish this wasn't happening but they just want to make Mom happy. Mom can convince herself this is purely an act of altruism, of motherly love. She's not asking anything for herself, of course. She is selflessly seeking the well-being of her sons.

She has a bumper sticker she's just waiting to put on her car: "My sons are honored disciples at Jesus' Elementary Discipleship School." In the ancient world, parents would sometimes gratify their own egos through the accomplishments of their children. Isn't that a weird culture? Can you even imagine a world in which parents would try to do that kind of thing? Mrs. Zebedee here is one of the first helicopter parents, swooping in to make sure her boys outshine all the other boys.

It's possible to be a parent and to be sucking the life out of your kids by gaining status through their achievements and in the process to deceive yourself, to make yourself think it's just about love and wanting them to do well. Sometimes I drive my children to go through open doors, but it's not about their advancement; it's really about my ego.

That's what's going on here. She kneels before Jesus. This is a posture of humility and surrender. In other words, it's possible to deceive yourself so that in an act of incredible entitlement and arrogance and grandiosity that everybody else can recognize, you actually think you're being and coming across as humble and self-effacing.

My drive to go through open doors reveals to me that mixture of a desire to serve God and a desire to serve my own ego. Not long ago I read online a "review" a woman had written after she had visited our church. She said, "I stood in the back and watched the speaker greet people, and his attitude was just move them in, move them out. He kept looking over people's shoulders at whoever came next. Somebody asked him for help, but he just gave them lip service and didn't really help at all."

When I read that, my first thought was, *I just feel bad she attended on a week someone else was preaching.* No, actually my first thought, honestly, was, *She doesn't know me, whoever this is. She doesn't know my temperament. She doesn't know how I'm wired. She doesn't know the demands on my time. She doesn't know my heart. Plus, she clearly decided not to like me or our church, so I can just reject her observations so I don't have to feel any pain about me.* That was my first thought.

I didn't have to strategize to do that. I didn't have to reflect to do that. It was just instinctive. But I know better. *Really, do I never do what she said? Do I always, or even consistently, genuinely love? Am I never or not often just gripped by my own little agenda and how I am doing? Am I really so humble and so free of self-promotion that indignation is the right response? Is it even sane?*

Waffle Boy—Clue Phone—it's for me.

The truth about me is I don't even *want* to know the truth about me. The truth about me is only God knows the truth about me. The truth about the truth is if I face the truth about me with Jesus, the truth will hurt me. In fact, it will kill me. But then, it will bring me life. Jesus said, "You will know the truth, and the truth will set you free"—but first, it will make you miserable.

Pursuing the open door will tell me the truth about what I'm really after.

What Is My Door Response Style?

We all have our own response tendencies when it comes to open doors. They fall into two broad categories: impulsives and resisters. Some people, when facing new opportunities, tend to focus on danger and risk and inadequacy and tend to shrink back. Their great need is for courage. Others love open doors— but they tend to jump through them without thinking ahead or counting the cost. Their great need is for discernment. Here's an inventory. See which side you tend to line up on:

IMPULSIVE	RESISTER
Activist	Contemplative
Tend to underthink	Tend to overthink
Move too fast	Move too slowly
Favorite saying: "He who hesitates is lost."	Favorite saying: "Look before you leap."
Favorite Bible verse: "Whatsoever you do, do it quickly."	Favorite Bible verse: "The Lord grants sleep to those he loves."
Favorite sins: sins of commission	Favorite sins: sins of omission
Strong will	Strong intellect
Distrust weakness	Distrust power

Both styles have strengths. Both styles have weaknesses. Whichever style is yours, if you are married, you probably married someone of the opposite style. That's true in my case. I won't tell you which is which, but my wife once bought a house I hadn't looked at yet. When we didn't have any money. Not that there's anything wrong with that.

The patron saint of impulsives might be Peter. He is naturally drawn to open doors. When invited to follow Jesus, he is the first one recorded to follow "immediately." He is the only disciple who jumps out of the boat to walk on water; he answers the call to defend Jesus even though slicing off a soldier's ear is not a strategic move. He often speaks before thinking—warning Jesus not to talk about being crucified, offering to build shrines to Moses and Elijah along with Jesus because "he did not know what to say" (Mark 9:6), instinctively promising to be faithful to Jesus no matter what even though he will deny him three times before dawn.

A prominent resister of open doors in the Bible might be Gideon. When we meet him, he is "threshing wheat in a winepress to keep it from the Midianites" (Judges 6:11). To thresh wheat in a winepress is like making a spoonful of coffee—it's a sign of his great timidity and fear.

When called by God, his immediate response is "But how can I save Israel? My clan is the weakest in Manasseh, and I am the least in my family" (Judges 6:15).

"But Lord, I just don't have a sense of peace about this."

If you are a resister, you face the temptation of rationalizing passivity and saying no to the open door of God. Famously, Gideon sets out a fleece before saying yes to God's call. This is one of the most misunderstood stories in the Bible. The fleece was not a sign of Gideon's faith. God had already called him—Gideon knew what he was supposed to do. The fleece was an expression of resistance. God responds to the fleece not as an affirmation of Gideon's faith but as a concession to Gideon's doubt.

If you're an impulsive, you will want to lean into wisdom. If you are an impulsive, you tend to lack discipline. You can be thoughtless, or insensitive to others, or driven by appetite. You may have a hard time with delayed gratification. You have a low frustration tolerance. You get bored easily. You can fly off the handle. Here are some suggestions for you:

- Ask counsel from wise friends before plunging forward with an idea.
- Cultivate relationships with people who are not only wise but strong enough to hold you accountable.
- Spend time praying about a potential open door before assuming that your intuition is a divine command.
- Study and read about an area of need before you commit yourself to action.
- When you come to the end of a season of activity, spend some time in reflection, perhaps with wise people you trust, so that you can become a wiser person before you go on to your next contest.
- Make a commitment, and then actually stick to it even when the next impulse, which looks so much more fun, comes along.

If you're a resister, what you most need is what you least want: another challenge. Another open door. Here are some suggestions for you:

- Fail at something. When it happens, let people know. Discover that failure isn't fatal.
- Try being wrong. Try letting other people know that sometimes you are wrong.
- Find a project so big that you know you cannot do it unless God is helping you. Commit to it.
- Hang around with some impulsive types. Watch how they take risks without actually dying. Real-life modeling is a great way to learn.
- Practice going through small doors. Compliment a stranger, volunteer for an extra assignment at work, write a letter to someone you admire (without including your credentials next to your name).
- Make a decision that's good enough instead of perfect. The next time you're at a hotel and the TV gets four hundred channels, just watch the first good show you run across, rather than monitoring all four hundred channels first so you can prove you watched the *best* show.
- Be scared. Obey God anyway.

Often we are paralyzed by decisions because of our fear that we'll not make a perfect one. As Lysa TerKeurst said to me, "God doesn't demand perfect decisions, just perfectly submitted ones." If we know our natural tendencies, we're equipped to better submit them to God.

What Do I Really Value?

In the early 1500s a young nobleman named Ignatius was defending a castle against a French invasion and had his leg shattered by a cannonball. While convalescing, he asked for some romance novels to read, but the only two books available to him were about the life of Christ and spiritual growth.

As he read these books, he learned a profound lesson about discerning God's will. While he was recovering his health, he had daydreams about his future. Sometimes he pictured himself having future courtly adventures and winning glory as a glamorous soldier. (He actually had his shattered leg rebroken and reset so it would look better in his courtly tights.) These daydreams were vivid and exciting in the moment. But he found that over time, when the vivid daydream had faded, the memory left him feeling flat and empty. Those daydreams of pursuing personal fame left a kind of aftertaste that was not in keeping with the person God was calling him to become.

At other times he began to dream about serving God. These dreams also were compelling when he had them. But he found that even after the vivid daydreams passed, he continued to feel joyful and happy in thinking about them. They did not have the same sour aftertaste that his dreams of personal glory had. He noticed this difference and came to conclude that God was calling him to serve as a spiritual guide and director rather than as a soldier.

His reflections on developing this awareness—an awareness of both our own spirit as well as of the ways God is moving within our spirit—were eventually written down in a resource called *The Spiritual Exercises*, and they have guided millions of people looking at open doors in the centuries since.[4] And his method of paying attention to the ways God is moving in our spirit is helpful even for choices that may not be about our vocations.

For example, some of the most important areas where God sets open doors before us involve friendship. Just as God opens doors for us to have impact, so God opens doors for us to have friends. But entering the friendship door also deserves discernment. There may be people in my life who are charming and fun to be with, and they may even say nice things to my face. But perhaps they pull me toward gossip or bitterness or cynicism or behaviors that I know are not my best self.

When I am walking through an open door and put myself on the line of actual commitments with real, live people, I test and discover whether the values I think I honor really hold sway in my life. Just as Ignatius did around his daydreams, I can reflect when I am apart from such people if being with them moves me toward or away from my best self.

Not long ago, Nancy and I were with two other couples that we have known for over thirty years. We live in different parts of the country now, but we were together in an intense way for several days. Several times during those days I would push the group toward being fully authentic with each other, to take the risk of honesty and transparency—to identify and seize relational open doors.

But then the spotlight turned to me, and the others said stuff like, "You know, John, intimacy is good. We like it. But sometimes you just force it. You always seem to feel this need to be the one asking questions or trying to make people respond to questions instead of just allowing conversation to happen, or you'll want to talk too much about what it is you're doing. You want to make things too much just about you." I looked at them. I've known all five people for more than thirty years. I have been good friends with a couple of them since the eighth grade.

I thought, *I'm going to have to get five brand-new friends who won't talk to me like this.*

Then Nancy and I talked for a long time afterward. Again, that got kind of bumpy at times, and at one point Nancy said, "You know, John, I love your friends, but sometimes I feel like I'm always having to enter your world and pay attention to your work and be with your friends, and you don't enter into my world nearly as much." I realized that as much as I said I valued truth telling, honesty, and authenticity, I didn't want to hear the truth about me, because the truth about me is I need to change in ways I don't want to change.

Now does this mean that when Nancy and I have a talk like this she's always right and I'm always wrong? Only God knows for sure. But I'm a pastor, so I'm close to God, so I probably have a much better shot at it.

The truth about me is I will never know what the truth about me is if I don't have some people close to me who love me and have courage. And I am aware—upon further review—that I want and need people in my life who love me enough to face pain in our relationship in order to call me to grow.

The apostle Paul writes, "Speaking the truth in love, we will in all things grow up into him who is the Head, that is, Christ" (Ephesians 4:15). Whom have you asked to speak the truth to you in love? And to whom are you doing that?

Our church is working on this as a staff, because we really are serious about wanting to live this from the inside out. Over a year ago we did an exercise called "The Fishbowl," and it has kind of become part of our vocabulary. We hired a coach to help us. She started by taking several weeks to have everybody in the circle prepare by writing down their most honest observations about one another so it would be in a really safe environment and we'd get really honest.

The next step was to speak about these privately with this coach, again, who was kind of this safe outside person. The next step was to have all of these written down on big poster sheets of paper, including some pretty raw material. Then we all gathered together, not for one day but for several days, from first thing in the morning until the end of our day, and we would put one person in the center of the room and have everybody tell that one person the most difficult-to-tell truths about their observations and concerns.

That's called "The Fishbowl," because a fish lives in transparent openness. There's just glass and water and light. You can see anything. Other animals don't. Bats are awake during the night; cats live under a bed with dead rodents that no one can see. Cats and bats prefer the darkness, but fish live in the light.

This is the fishbowl. Our coach said to me, "By the way, you're the leader, so it starts with you. You have to be in the fishbowl first, and you have to be in the fishbowl longer than anybody else on the team." So I sat in the fishbowl for several hours.

Jesus said a long time ago that before we go around identifying splinters in other people's eyes, we ought to remove the logs from our own. And there's always a log. I learned far more from my time in the middle of the fishbowl than from the (more comfortable) hours when other people were in it.

God calls us to the adventure of the open door. We are to go through these doors for the sake of others.

On the other side, we will discover the hard truth about ourselves, and that truth is not often flattering. We are—every one of us—"little strengths" on our own power. But the God who opens the door is the God who gives us strength to go through it. When we go, we find we're not just entering new territory. We're becoming new people.

CHAPTER 8

THE JONAH COMPLEX

And the word of the Lord came to Jonah: "You shall go to the city of
Nineveh; you shall summon all the skill and energies that I have placed
at your disposal to do a great work in that city, and you shall proclaim
my word with courage and passion, and people will respond and good
will triumph and lives will change and a city will be renewed through
what I will do with you."

And Jonah said, "No, thanks."

And Jonah said, "Let's have Nahum try it. Nahum will try
anything."

And Jonah said, "What time does that ship leave for Tarshish?"

GOD IS THE GOD OF OPEN DOORS. He opens doors all around,
boundless opportunities to contribute to humanity in ways
large and small, to make our lives count for eternity. Who
could not want that?

I could not want that.

I long for open doors, yet I resist going through them. I shrink back on the threshold. I don't see them. Or seeing them, I don't walk through them.

Abraham Maslow called this strange tendency we have to run away from our destiny "the Jonah complex." It is an evasion of growth, a defense against calling. "If you deliberately plan to be less than you are capable of being, then I warn you that you'll be deeply unhappy for the rest of your life. You will be evading your own capacities, your own possibilities."[1]

Because of this, he said, we also have a mixed response to others who actually do say a wholehearted yes to God's call on their lives. "We surely love and admire all the persons who have incarnated the true, the good, the beautiful, the just, the perfect, the ultimately successful. And yet they also make us uneasy, anxious, confused, perhaps a little jealous or envious, a little inferior, clumsy."[2]

Every time God opens a door for someone in Scripture, there is a little tug-of-war. He calls, the one called resists for one reason or another, and then there is a decision. Most often, since the Bible is God's story, the one God calls eventually says yes. Sometimes, as with the Rich Young Ruler, the door is rejected.

In all the Bible's stories, perhaps the tale of Jonah is the most famous and colorful example of someone running from his or her divine destiny. Phillip Cary, in a wonderful commentary on Jonah, says the narrative is laid out in such a way that it uniquely leaves each of us having to figure out our own response to God.³ One of the problems with Jonah is that a lot of us think we know his story, but we don't. ·

The average person usually associates Jonah with one other character; they will think of it as the story of Jonah and the whale. The whale's name is Monstro, and Jonah is running away from Geppetto and wants to be a real boy, and . . . people get a little fuzzy at that point.

But Jonah is really "the patron saint of refused callings."⁴ His story remains unforgettable because it is the greatest picture in all biblical literature of saying no to God's open door. In his story we see all our evasions of God's calling mirrored back to us. In turning to Jonah now, we learn the reasons why we're tempted to say no to God so that we might learn to say yes instead.

Fear Holds Us Back

"The word of the LORD came to Jonah son of Amittai: 'Go to the great'"—that word *great* will come up again—"'city of Nineveh and preach against it, because its wickedness has come up before me'" (Jonah 1:1-2).

Jonah was a prophet; he was not a priest. Priests served in the Temple. They offered sacrifices. They led worship. A prophet was different. A prophet was a reformer. A prophet was an activist—kind of a gadfly, kind of a troublemaker. Prophets were always pricking people's consciences. Israel always had a lot of priests but generally just one prophet at a time because that was all Israel could stand.

One day the word of the Lord comes to this prophet

Jonah. When you hear from God, and sometimes you will, it may be only a few words, but they can change your life.

Life isn't easy when you're a prophet. The word of the Lord comes to Jonah:

> *Could you, would you go to preach?*
> *Could you, would you go to reach*
> *The people in Assyria?*
> *For you fit my criteria.*

And Jonah says to the Lord:

> *I would not go there in a boat.*
> *I would not go there in a float.*
>
> *I would not go there in a gale.*
> *I would not go there in a whale.*
>
> *I do not like the people there.*
> *If they all died, I would not care.*
>
> *I will not go to that great town.*
> *I'd rather choke. I'd rather drown.*
>
> *I will not go by land or sea.*
> *So stop this talk and let me be.*

Jonah was a prophet, but he was a prophet to Israel. He had nothing to do with other countries. They didn't have Scripture. They didn't have a Temple. They didn't know about sacrifices. They didn't know God. Word comes to him, "Go to Nineveh and preach." It's striking how this is expressed. Not "Go to Nineveh and preach *to* it"; "Go to Nineveh and preach *against* it," the text says. That's a daunting task.

Nineveh was the capital of Assyria. In the seventh and eighth centuries BC, Assyria was *the* great world power. It chewed up and spit out countries right and left. It would put the populations of countries that it defeated on death marches. It practiced genocide as state policy. When Israel was split into two sections, there was the northern kingdom of ten tribes and the southern kingdom of just two tribes. The northern kingdom was captured and basically vaporized, basically obliterated, by Assyria.

Nineveh was hated so much that the prophet Nahum named it "the city of blood." That's what it was called. That was its title. "Woe to the city of blood, full of lies, full of plunder, never without victims! . . . Piles of dead." Now you think about this: "Bodies without number, people stumbling over the corpses" (Nahum 3:1, 3).

Nahum predicts the fall of Nineveh: "Your wound is fatal. All who hear the news about you clap their hands at your fall, for who has not felt your endless cruelty?" (Nahum 3:19). Nineveh is so hated, not just for cruelty, but for *endless* cruelty. When it is destroyed, Nahum says, people are going to clap. They are going to stand up and cheer.

Nahum said very strong, condemning words about Nineveh, but where do you think Nahum was when he said those words?

He was in Israel.

Then the word of the Lord comes to Jonah: "Go to Nineveh. Learn to speak Assyrian, and tell them face-to-face that they're facing judgment."

Jonah says, "Lord, Nahum got to taunt them from a distance. Couldn't we, like, send them a telegram or something?"

The word of the Lord came to Jonah. How did the word come? Was it a burning bush? Was it a still, small voice? Was it an angel? Was it a vision? Was it a dream? Was there room for doubt? The text doesn't say.

Did people around Jonah know? Was there a Mrs. Jonah? Did Jonah go home and have her ask, "How was work today?" And tell her, "Well, I'm supposed to go to Assyria and condemn them face-to-face," and have her say, "You've got to be crazy"? The text doesn't say. It just says the word of the Lord came to Jonah, "Go to Nineveh."

What we do know is that God had opened a door for Jonah, and Jonah not only didn't go through it but ran the other way, and the implication is that he did this because he was afraid. "I'm very brave generally, only today I happen to have a headache," said Tweedledum in Lewis Carroll's *Through the Looking Glass.*[5]

God said to Jonah, "I have set before you an open door. It leads to Nineveh." Jonah would have gone, but he had a headache.

Sometimes open doors are not fun. Sometimes they're not even safe. Always they're about something greater than our own benefit. Often they lead to Nineveh.

Nineveh is the place God calls you where you do not want to go. Nineveh is trouble. Nineveh is danger. Nineveh is fear. What do you do when God says to you, "Go to Nineveh; go to the place you do not want to go"? Because God will say that to you.

Now Jonah arises in response to the word of the Lord. He does leave home, but not for Nineveh. He heads for Tarshish.

It may happen like this: I know God is asking me to go to Nineveh. I know God wants me to confront this person, have a conversation about the truth, but that would be hard. That would be unpleasant. I don't want to face that pain, so I'll just go to Tarshish.

I know God is calling me to serve in this area, but I don't want to. It might be humbling. It might be difficult. It might be scary. I don't want to do that, so I'll run away to Tarshish.

I know God has called me to teach or counsel or build or lead or invite or give, but I might fail. It might be hard. I might be anxious. So I'll get on a ship bound for Tarshish.

But here's what matters: fear is never overcome by situation avoidance. We were born to be brave. The consistent command to us is the command that came to a fearful leader named Joshua: "Be strong and courageous . . . for the LORD your God will be with you" (Joshua 1:9). Three times in the first chapter of the book of Jonah we're told that Jonah runs—not just from his calling but "from the presence of the LORD" (1:3, NRSV). Yet the antidote to fear is the presence of God.

Having Other Options Holds Us Back

Jonah goes down to Joppa, which is a port city, where he finds a ship bound for Tarshish. "After paying the fare, he went aboard and sailed for Tarshish to flee from the LORD" (Jonah 1:3).

A little detail that we might skip over nowadays is the text says Jonah *paid* the fare. This is a big deal. In Jonah's day, money was still relatively new. The ancient world used a barter economy, and money was tremendously scarce among the people of Israel. Hardly anybody would be able to do what Jonah did.

Jonah had money enough to buy passage for a long voyage out of his pocket. He had mobility; he had options. Here's one of the dangerous things about money: having money makes it easier for us to think we can run away from God, because we've got options. Sometimes it's hard for a prophet and a profit to coexist.

I think of a man I know who loves to teach, who has a passion for children to be able to learn. If he would have allowed his passion for education to reveal divine doors in his life, he would have made a fabulous grade school teacher.

But he is from a family of Highly Successful People. His parents would have been a little embarrassed for him to be "just a teacher." "You should explore other options," they told him.

Having "options" of making more money and obtaining a higher-status title actually got in the way of what could have been his dream calling. He ended up making lots more money than he would have had he become a teacher. He just missed out on his life.

He got an MBA. But it was from the University of Tarshish.

When I was in seventh grade, there was a girl in our class I'll call Shirley. She was awkward; she wore the wrong clothes. She had red hair and freckles and buckteeth. No one sat next to her at lunch; no one invited her to be on their team.

I could have done those things. I could have been her friend. Or I could have at least gone out of my way to be kind to her. But I didn't. I suppose I was afraid that if I did, I might have been as rejected as she was. I wasn't the most popular kid in the class, but I wasn't as lowly as Shirley, and I wasn't willing to give up what status I had to befriend her.

I was running to Tarshish.

Tarshish is significant, not just because it's in the opposite direction from Nineveh, but because in many ways it was the opposite kind of city.

Nineveh was a military city. Tarshish was not a military power, but it had great wealth. It was a pioneer in trade. Commerce over the sea was kind of like new technology and was making some people rich. Not a bad thing necessarily, but it has a way of leading to greed and arrogance and pride. So that phrase—"a ship of Tarshish"—became a symbol of wealth in the ancient world.

It actually comes up a number of times in the Old Testament. Isaiah says, "The LORD of hosts has a day against all that is proud and lofty, against all that is lifted up and high; . . . against all the ships of Tarshish. . . . The haughtiness of people shall be humbled" (Isaiah 2:12, 16-17, NRSV).

A similar image is used in Ezekiel: "The ships of Tarshish serve as carriers for your wares. . . . With your great wealth and your wares you enriched the kings of the earth. Now you are shattered by the sea" (Ezekiel 27:25, 33-34).

The ships of Tarshish became symbols of wealth and self-sufficiency and power and greed. Is it hard to imagine that once a group of human beings was so deluded that they thought technology, wealth, and a clever economic system could make them secure?

Jonah ran away to Wall Street. Jonah ran away to Madison Avenue. Jonah ran away to Silicon Valley. Jonah gets on the ship of Tarshish. People have been headed for that ship for a long time. Jonah thinks he's running toward safety, but maybe what really looks safe from a human perspective is not actually safe at all. Maybe the only safe place is to be in the will of God for your life, even if it means choosing the door to Nineveh, that scary place you don't want to go.

Blindness to the Door in Front of Us Holds Us Back

Jonah's boat sets out to sea. Another door will open to him, but it will be heavily disguised.

"Then the LORD sent a great wind on the sea, and such a violent [literally, 'great'] storm arose"—it's the same word that described the great city of Nineveh, but now it's God doing great things, sending a great wind and a great storm—"that the ship threatened to break up. All the sailors were afraid and each cried out to his own god. And they threw the cargo into the sea to lighten the ship" (Jonah 1:4-5).

These are professional sailors. They don't panic easily, but they panic now. In the ancient world when life was short, a long voyage like this could take years. It could be your one chance for great wealth. The sailors are throwing all their hopes into the sea, each praying to his own god. In their world each tribal or ethnic group had its own god. We sometimes think we invented multiculturalism, but this is a very diverse, multicultural crew, displaying a vibrant religious pluralism. Each one prayed to his own god.

When the sea is calm, any old name for any old god is okay. But when a storm hits, everything changes, and now you're hoping one of those gods turns out to be real.

Meanwhile, Jonah is missing the great open door of his life, sleeping in the bottom of the boat. When I think about this part of the story, I think about a time when I took my daughter whale watching. I love whales, but I don't do very well in boats. I get seasick. So when I took Mallory to go whale watching, I took multiple Dramamine tablets before we got on the boat, and I had Mallory do the same.

I was so sleepy, I fell asleep and drooled on the deck of that boat. Everybody was watching us. I ended up pouring coffee down me and tea down Mallory trying to get us awake, and finally there was a whale. We saw its tail, and I said, "Oh, Mal, look—a whale" and then went back to sleep and slept all the way into port.

Jonah is sleeping in a turbulent boat without the aid of

Dramamine, and the captain is stunned. He says to Jonah, "How can you sleep?" I love the old King James Version of this: "What meanest thou, O sleeper?" It's what the captain says to Jonah. "What are you thinking?" "Get up and call on your god! Maybe he will take notice of us so that we will not perish" (Jonah 1:6).

Now this is tremendous irony. The pagan Gentile ship captain is calling the man of God to prayer. The pagan is doing what prophets do—issuing a call to pray. The prophet is doing what pagans do—sleeping when it's prayer time. God is up to something.

Jonah confesses nothing, so the sailors cast lots to identify the problem, and the lots indicate that the problem is Jonah.

So the sailors ask him, "What's your story?" Jonah answers, "I am a Hebrew and I worship the LORD, the God of heaven, who made the sea and the dry land" (Jonah 1:9). This terrified them. Literally, the text says, "And the people feared a great fear." (That word *great* again.) It's ambiguous: perhaps the sailors feared an enormous fear, perhaps a redemptive fear, "and they asked, 'What have you done?' (They knew he was running away from the LORD, because he had already told them so.)" (verse 10).

The parenthesis tells us something wonderful is happening, and the writer tips us off by the language he uses for God. In the Hebrew Scriptures three main words are used to refer to the Divine. *Elohim* was the generic word, usually translated "God." This word could refer to any gods of any tribes. *Adonai* is often translated "Lord"; in the ancient world it was a general title of respect for one in authority. *YHWH* was the most holy and sacred name, for it is the name God used to reveal himself to his people. It was so sacred that eventually pious Jews would not even pronounce it. In most English translations, when *Lord* is spelled with all capital letters, it translates YHWH. This name is not generic; it refers only to the God of Israel.

In this story the sailors prayed each to their own *elohim*.

But Jonah tells them about YHWH—the God who tells people his name, who wants to be known, who created the seas and the lands. That's language all Gentiles would know.

Now this is the reason for the parenthesis in the text. The sailors already know that Jonah is running away from his god. They figure that it's just a tribal god of Israel. But they are told there is one great God. They are told his name. They see his power. And they fear with a great fear.

They are coming to know Jonah's God, on this ship of Tarshish in the middle of a storm. One of the reasons that they are going to believe Jonah is that he comes to them as a screwup, as a knucklehead, as a mistake. He had been a prophet all these years. This will be the greatest mass Gentile conversion he has ever seen, and it is Jonah's failure that God uses to bring these people to faith. Whatever else this book is, it is not a story about a human plan. It is an "opened" door, and we are not the openers.

Sometimes I'm running away from Nineveh, and a door opens up on a ship of Tarshish. Sometimes I fail to go through open doors because I don't recognize their presence.

Chuck Colson is disgraced and sent to prison, and he finds doors opening to ministry there that never opened to him in the White House. Helen Keller faces severe disabilities, yet a door is opened to her precisely because of them to help untold millions. A Sunday school teacher named Rosa Parks is told to sit in the back of a bus, and her quiet refusal opens the door to the conscience of a nation.

A woman at our church said to an eight-year-old boy who was all dressed up on Easter morning, "You look so handsome. Did you get that outfit for Easter?"

No, the little fellow explained. He got it for the funeral of his daddy, who had just died a few weeks ago.

It turns out that this woman also lost her father when she was eight years old. She got down on her knees, took him in her arms, and spoke to him as the only one in his world who knew exactly how he felt.

How many open doors are all around me—someone feels alone, someone waits to be inspired, someone is aching with rejection, someone is racked with guilt—just waiting for me to pay attention?

Our Sense of Guilt or Inadequacy May Hold Us Back

The sailors ask Jonah, "What should we do to you to make the sea calm down for us?" Jonah responds, "Pick me up and throw me into the sea . . . and it will become calm. I know that it is my fault that this great storm has come upon you" (Jonah 1:11-12). Jonah is going to stop running, but he thinks his story is over because of the mistake he has made.

Arthur Kemp's story is recorded in a book called *God's Yes Was Louder than My No: Rethinking the African American Call to Ministry.* His family had predicted he would become a preacher when he was very young, and when he was a young man, he sensed clearly God saying to him, "Go feed my sheep." He recognized it as a call to preach. But he got in a ship bound for Tarshish.

He spent the next decade of his life trying to prove how unworthy he was. "I determined that I was going to be the worst possible human being you could be, to make myself unfit to be a minister."[6] He wasn't a drinking man, but he started to drink; wasn't a gambler but learned how; and he began drug dealing and pimping, all as a way of running from his calling.

For him, Tarshish was living on the streets and losing all self-respect. Until he went to a prayer meeting one night and the storm broke and he sobbed, "I've got to preach, I've got to preach," and the pastor told him he would not have any peace until he did.

God's yes is louder than my no.

But Jonah's no is pretty loud. He tells the sailors to throw him over.

Amazingly, the sailors don't do it. "The men did their best to row back to land. But they could not, for the sea grew even wilder than before" (Jonah 1:13). Their lives are at stake, but they don't want to sacrifice the life of this Hebrew stranger. It's amazing, because these are the Hebrew Scriptures. These sailors on the ship of Tarshish have more compassion, more raw humanity, on the Hebrew prophet than the Hebrew prophet had on the people of Nineveh.

You have to be really careful about judging who the good guys are and who the bad guys are, who is on God's side and who is not on God's side.

Now the sailors hold a prayer meeting: "They cried out to the LORD, 'Please, LORD, do not let us die for taking this man's life. Do not hold us accountable for killing an innocent man, for you, LORD, have done as you pleased'" (Jonah 1:14).

Three times they call him YHWH by name, the writer hitting us over the head just in case we the readers are a little slow.

They take him to the side of the boat.

Imagine this moment. Awesome storm, terrified sailors, runaway prophet, capsizing boat. His body is thrown into the water. On the deck, all of a sudden, everything is calm. The storm is gone.

"At this the men greatly feared the LORD." There's that word again. "And they offered a sacrifice to the LORD"— that's an act of worship—"and made vows to him," as an act of commitment, an act of devotion (Jonah 1:16).

This pagan boat becomes a place of worship. The ship of Tarshish becomes a temple of the living God. That wasn't Jonah's plan. It turns out that the sailors on this ship are not bit players in this story after all. This is not some little throwaway thing in a story about Nineveh. It turns out that God's story is so big, it's also a story about Tarshish. It turns out that Jonah thought he would thwart what God wanted to do. It turns out that God is at work in ways that Jonah cannot even begin to dream of.

Jonah's closed door to God becomes God's open door to the sailors.

If Dr. Seuss were summarizing the story so far, it would go something like this:

God says, "Go."
Jonah says, "No."
God says, "Blow."
Jonah says, "So?"
The captain says, "Bro."
Jonah says, "Throw."
The sailors say, "Whoa!"
So they tossed Jonah in and he sank very low,
But God had more places for Jonah to go.

We Miss Doors When We Miss Prayer

We've heard the story too often. So imagine what it is like to hear it for the very first time. Jonah is sinking into the sea, but the Lord "appointed" a great fish to swallow Jonah.

Jonah was inside the fish three days and three nights. If that doesn't strike you as at least a little funny, something is wrong with your sense of joy, and you'll need that for open-door living.

This word *appointed* could be translated "commissioned." It is a governing word. It is what a king would do if he were appointing an ambassador or a messenger or something. But it's used here for a fish. God says, "Hey, Fish." The fish says, "Yes, Lord?" God says, "Go pick up Jonah. Directions will be given on a need-to-know basis. This is important: swallow, don't chew. I'll tell you where to drop him off." The fish says, "Okay, Lord." This fish is better at taking orders than God's prophet.

The primary word associated with God in the story is the word *great*. It starts by God saying to Jonah, "I want you to go to the *great* city of Nineveh," because it turns out that God has a great heart, because it turns out God has a heart for the great city. Then Jonah runs the other way, so the Bible says God sends a *great* wind, and it produces a *great* storm. Then these pagan sailors are converted through a *great* fear. Then God appoints a fish for Jonah—it's described as a *great* fish.

Jonah, on the other hand, messes everything up. If the main word for God in this book is *great*, the main word for Jonah is *down*.

God says, "Go to Nineveh," and Jonah goes *down* to Joppa. Then he goes in a ship *down* to Tarshish. Then, in the ship, he goes *down* into the bottom, where he sleeps. Then he goes *down* into the water in the storm. Then he goes *down* into the fish. Jonah has hit bottom.

For an Israelite, you don't get lower than this. The sea was a place of great fear, great terror. A place of death.

A great fish is not the particular mode of transportation that Jonah had in mind when he was leaving Joppa. But he is given the opportunity to learn something about the strange, troubling, hilarious grace of God.

Never look a gift whale in the mouth.

From the guts of the fish, Jonah prays. He says, "In my distress I called to the LORD, and he answered me. From deep in the realm of the dead I called for help, and you listened to my cry" (Jonah 2:2).

He didn't pray about his call to Nineveh, or his flight to Tarshish, or the storm on the boat. He did not talk to God at all until he ended up in a fish.

Why did Jonah pray in the fish?

Because he had nothing better to do.

God brings Jonah down, down, down, down to a place of desperation in a fish in the sea. The honest truth is he turns to God because he has nowhere else to turn. The whole first chapter of the story of Jonah is human action. Jonah makes plans. Jonah has resources. Jonah is going places . . . and it is a disaster. And then the storm hits, and Jonah's story grinds to a halt.

In the second chapter of Jonah, there is no action at all. Just prayer. And then the good stuff starts to happen for Jonah.

When the apostle Paul wants open doors, the place he starts is prayer. Open doors are interactions between heaven and earth, and that's why they start in prayer.

If I want an adventure with God, I can start by praying today for open doors. "God, would you open doors of encouragement, doors of opportunity, doors of possibility, doors of generosity today? God, make this day a day of the open door."

I don't have to wait until I hit bottom.

It's interesting that the Bible has one other shipwreck story—about Paul, in Acts 27—that is almost the exact opposite of Jonah's. Jonah is running away from his calling to preach to the dangerous capital of Assyria; Paul is running toward his calling of preaching to the dangerous capital of Rome. Jonah's presence on the boat puts the sailors at risk; Paul's presence on the boat is their salvation. Paul cries out to God for open doors when he's safe; Jonah cries out to God for safety when he hits bottom.

All too often, we don't call out to God *until* we hit bottom.

An old children's song is called "There's a Hole in the Bottom of the Sea." It's all about a child's delight in obscurity and hiddenness. "There's is a wing on the flea on the fly on a limb on a log in a hole in the bottom of the sea. . . . "

Here's the story of Jonah. There's a man in the guts of a fish in a storm by a boat in the bottom of the sea. And he discovers . . . there is God. Even if we wait until we hit bottom to pray, God is there.

Jonah prays, God hears, God opens a door, and Jonah gets delivered, but what happens next is so goofy, so slapstick, I wouldn't mention it except it's in the Bible, so we have to talk about it.

Jonah gets delivered on the third day. The third day is a common framework for God's rescue in the Bible, so a reader would expect that Jonah is going to get some dramatic rescue event. A visitation from the angel Gabriel, a ride home on a chariot of fire, an instantaneous teleportation. Something like that.

Not in this story.

"The LORD commanded the fish, and it vomited Jonah onto dry land" (Jonah 2:10). Is it just me, or is that a little more detail than we really want? This is like the sixth-grade version of the story.

If you wonder why the English translators of the Bible did not choose a more dignified, churchier word than *vomit*, it is because the Hebrew word is even more graphic than our English word.

The writer wants to make sure the reader gets this. Jonah did not get dropped off by an angel. The whale had a protein spill, tossed his cookies, lost his lunch, launched the food shuttle, took a ride on the Regurgitron.

Jonah ends up on the shore. Not a tragic figure, covered with suffering. Not a heroic figure, covered with glory. A ridiculous figure, covered with shrimp cocktail and tuna tartare.

The most basic way you can divide all stories is like this: every story is either a tragedy—joy loses, life loses, hope loses; or it is a comedy—joy wins, life wins, hope wins.

Jonah is a comedy.

Jonah keeps going down, but then these funny things keep happening. Jonah, who ought to be the hero of the story, told by God to go east, runs west. A prophet, who ought to know better, thinks he can flee from God by sailing to Tarshish. A Gentile captain calls the man of God to pray. Pagan sailors, who in the ancient world were not noted for their piety, get converted to the God of Israel. Jonah thinks he is going to drown, and God sends a fish, like an Enterprise rental car pickup/delivery vehicle, for him.

And in case anybody hasn't caught on yet, the writer throws in a regurgitation scene.

It turns out that when human beings are going down, down, down, God is up to something great, and from God's perspective, death and the grave are not a problem at all. Human rebellion and stubbornness are not a problem.

God laughs at it all. God laughs at death, laughs at the grave. Jonah ends up vomited onto the shore.

One day we will understand that joy wins. Jonah is a joy book. It is comic in the most sublime, transcendent, wonderful sense of that word because there is another character between every line in this book.

Jonah, we are told, is from a town called Gath-hepher, which is a few miles away from Nazareth. Another prophet would come from Nazareth, would fall asleep on the boat while everyone else panicked, and would still the storm by his response.

Jonah's name means "the dove," which is a name that means "was given to a beloved one." Another prophet would go down into the water, come up out of the water, and see a dove descending, hearing a voice from heaven call him beloved.

Jesus said toward the end of his life he had one sign to give this sorry world, and he called it the sign of Jonah. "As Jonah was three days and three nights in the belly of a huge fish, so the Son of Man will be three days and three nights in the heart of the earth" (Matthew 12:40).

The early church used to meet in a place called the catacombs. Tombs, underground burial places. The first art inspired by Jesus was not art that appeared in great cathedrals or on enormous frescoes; it was art that was drawn, etched, carved in tombs, in the hidden catacombs. The Old Testament figure found most frequently is not Abraham or Moses or David.

It's Jonah.

Why? Because the early church got the joke.

Joy wins.

And the turning point in the story comes when Jonah turns to God in prayer. He turns to God because he has nowhere else to turn. But God is not proud. He accepts even those who come to him as a last resort. "Knock and the door will be opened to you" (Matthew 7:7).

Lack of Love Will Keep Us from Entering Open Doors

But the story of Jonah doesn't end on that note. It's left on a strange, unresolved, discordant note. For a reason.

There's a possibly legendary story that Johann Sebastian Bach's wife was once playing the harpsichord while he was in bed, and she kept an unresolved seventh chord, which bothered him so much he couldn't sleep. We don't know why she did this. She had twenty children—maybe she didn't have time to practice. Maybe she knew it would bother Johann and she wanted to get back at him for making her have twenty children. He finally got up out of bed, sat down at the harpsichord, and played the appropriate resolved chord so he could sleep.

The dissonant word in the Jonah story is the word *evil*. God tells Jonah to go preach against Nineveh "for their evil has come up before me" (Jonah 1:2, ESV).

Something is off with God's world. It keeps God up at night.

Jonah does not really want to go to Nineveh for one reason: Jonah does not like the Ninevites.

God places an open door before Jonah—but it isn't mostly about Jonah. It is a door for Jonah to be a vehicle of divine love for someone else. It is his lack of love that allows him to run the other way.

It is love that pushes a mother and father through the door of sacrifice to take responsibility for a little life.

It is love that draws a high-powered lawyer like Gary Haugen to give up money to bet everything on International Justice Mission.

It is love that gives the widow's mite, that keeps no record of wrongs, that honors the promise of marriage when doing so is hard, that listens to the grieving friend.

The real reason Jonah does not want to walk through God's open door is this simple: a failure of love.

So he goes to Nineveh when it is clear the alternative is to become a living sushi bar. He preaches a message, but his message may be the lamest in all the Bible: "Forty more days and Nineveh will be overthrown" (Jonah 3:4).

This is maybe the worst sermon of all time. No mention of God or repentance or mercy. No illustration, no application, no edification. Jonah is putting no effort into this at all. He's phoning it in.

But the strangest thing happens. People listen. They begin to respond. Their response is so widespread that everyone from the king all the way down to the poorest and weakest citizen repents, and even the animals wear sackcloth.

Which tells us that our adequacy or lack of it is never the issue when God opens a door. "I know that your strength is small. . . . "

God sees Nineveh's repentance and is filled with compassion. "When God saw what they did and how they turned from their evil ways, he relented" (Jonah 3:10).

Jonah looks at all this, and you would think he'd be thrilled.

"But all this was grievous to Jonah, a great evil, and he was very angry."[7]

Jonah can't take it. Now *Jonah* can't sleep. He looks at Nineveh repenting and being forgiven by God, and he says, "This is evil." Not just evil, "*great* evil." This is the only time in the story that these two words are brought together, and there is a reason for this. What is great to God—grace to Nineveh—is great evil to Jonah.

[Jonah] prayed to the LORD, "Isn't this what I said, LORD, when I was still at home? That is what I tried to forestall by fleeing to Tarshish. I knew that you are a gracious and compassionate God, slow to anger and abounding in love, a God who relents from sending calamity. Now, LORD, take away my life, for it is better for me to die than to live." (Jonah 4:2-3)

In fact, Jonah didn't say anything like this back home in the first chapter. The implication there was that he ran away out of fear. Now he conveniently remembers himself as the champion of justice. He claims he always knew God was going to go soft.

It turns out I may not even have clarity about why I say no to God's open doors. I may misremember in ways that make me look braver than I really was. I may need help from God and from people who know me well to look at why I suffer from the Jonah complex.

One of the numerous ways that Jonah is unique among prophets is this: his lack of empathy. Every other prophet not only pleads with people on behalf of God, they plead with God on behalf of the people. The anguish of the people causes other prophets anguish. They identify with the very people they have to declare judgment upon.

Not Jonah.

Declaring judgment is easy for him. He wants to run from the door because he doesn't really love the people that the door will lead him to.

Lack of love makes it easy for me to say no to the door.

A Wrong View of God Will Cause Me to Miss Open Doors

There's something else going on in this prayer that would be very apparent to its readers: "I knew that you are a gracious and compassionate God."

Jonah is quoting here the most famous confession of

God's identity in the history of Israel, when God revealed himself to Moses on Mount Sinai.

What God actually said was that he is "the gracious and compassionate God, slow to anger, abounding in love *and truth*" (Exodus 34:6, my translation).

Jonah's omission would be screamingly obvious to any Israelite reading the story. This would be like if you were at a wedding ceremony and the groom said: "I take you to be my wedded spouse, for better or worse, in sickness and in health, for richer."

Jonah leaves out *truth*. Jonah is impugning the character of God. He believes God is not reliable. I will never trust God to go through open doors if I think he is unfaithful.

All God says in return is, "Is it right for you to be angry?" (Jonah 4:4).

Jonah doesn't answer. Jonah gives God the silent treatment. Jonah is apparently part Swedish.

Jonah runs away again, east of the city, and waits hopefully for the city to be blasted.

Then the LORD God provided a leafy plant and made it grow up over Jonah to give shade for his head to ease his discomfort, and Jonah was very happy about the plant. But at dawn the next day God provided a worm, which chewed the plant so that it withered. When the sun rose, God provided a scorching east wind, and the sun blazed on Jonah's head so that he grew faint. He wanted to

die, and said, "It would be better for me to die than
to live."

But God said to Jonah, "Is it right for you to be
angry about the plant?"

"It is," he said. "And I'm so angry I wish I were
dead." (Jonah 4:6-9)

This is about something deeper than getting a sunburn.
Prophets were performance artists in their day. Because
people often ignore words, God would have prophets act
out their message in shocking ways. Always the prophet was
the actor and Israel the audience.

Except here.

In this little drama, God is the actor. God sends a plant,
God sends a worm, and God sends the wind. Jonah is the
audience. What's happening here is God wants to save Jonah.

For Jonah has gone east of the city. "East" was the direction of the enemies of Israel—east of Eden after the Fall, east
where the murderous Cain went.

God sends shade. That is full of meaning for an Israelite
reader.

Psalm 17:8-9 reads, "Hide me in the shadow [the *shade*]
of your wings from the wicked who are out to destroy me,
from my mortal enemies who surround me."

Shade means to be under God's protection. Literally, the
text says the shade was to deliver him from evil.

When the plant goes up, literally what the text says is
"And Jonah rejoiced in the plant with great joy." To Jonah,

it's not just about physical protection. To Jonah, when the plant goes up, it means Nineveh is going down. God is going to protect his people. God is going to destroy their enemies. That's why Jonah rejoices in the plant "with great joy." He is rejoicing in the destruction of the people he hates. Nineveh is going down.

God doesn't look at categories the way I do and think, *People in this category, they're my kind of people. I like these kinds of people. But people in that category over there, I can let go of them without much pain.* People matter to God. Depressed people. Educated people. Divorced people. People with different politics from yours. They matter to God. Conservative people and liberal people. Muslims. Atheists. New Age people. Every color of skin. Asian people. Hispanic people. Caucasian people. African American people. Gay people. Old people. People matter to God. Every one of them.

God says to Jonah, "You have been concerned about this plant, though you did not tend it or make it grow. . . . And should I not have concern for the great city of Nineveh, in which there are more than a hundred and twenty thousand people who cannot tell their right hand from their left—and also many animals?" (Jonah 4:10-11).

The story just ends with Jonah sitting there. Doesn't that drive you a little crazy? Isn't that a really crummy way to end the story? Why would a writer do that?

Actually, another storyteller will do the same thing. Jesus ends the story of the Prodigal Son exactly like the book of

Jonah, with a rebel saved by grace and a loving father appealing to a self-righteous pouter.

It's not that the storyteller can't think up the ending.

It's that this story isn't about Jonah. It's about us and our response to God.

A great artist knows that when you leave a story unresolved, people can't just walk away and dismiss it. They've got to keep working it out. Like Bach's chord, it keeps them up.

That's the idea.

There's a door out there with your name on it. Right now. It's open.

What will you do?

CHAPTER 9

THANK GOD FOR CLOSED DOORS

"Every time God closes a door, somebody somewhere gets ticked off."
    "Every time God closes a door, somebody decides they know better and want to trade places with him."
    "Every time God closes a door, he's up to something."

BASEBALL EXECUTIVES say some of the greatest trades are the ones never made. Similarly, some of the greatest prayers are the ones that never get answered the way we want. Some of the greatest doors are those that never get opened.

The Bible is as full of closed doors as it is of open ones: the door to Eden was closed after the Fall. The door to the ark was closed in judgment. The door to the Promised Land was closed to Moses. The door to building the Temple was closed to David.

The letter to the church in Philadelphia in Revelation says that it is in the power of the holy one not only to open doors that no one can shut but also to shut doors that no one can open.

But I generally don't like or understand closed doors.

If someone were to ask, "What is the single biggest motivator for prayer?" I suppose in a single phrase the response would be "Answered prayer." When we pray and God answers; when there is a need and God gives really clear direction; when someone has been ill in body or spirit for years and people pray and healing comes; when we feel anxious and are visited by peace; when we need an idea and an idea is given; when in response to prayer a marriage gets rescued or a runaway child comes home or someone lands a job or finds a place to live, it makes us want to pray more.

If somebody were to ask, "What's the single biggest de-motivator for prayer?" I suppose that could be answered in two words as well: "Unanswered prayer." Somebody would love to be married, and they pray for years to meet the right person, but they never do. Or somebody wrestles with depression, and they ask God for it to lift, and it doesn't. Or somebody gets seriously cheated or wronged in their work, and they ask God for justice to prevail, and justice does not prevail.

Ogden Nash wrote that a door is that which a dog is perpetually on the wrong side of. No creature on earth wants to feel shut out on the wrong side of a door. Closed doors discourage us. They may come up in a job or a relationship or our financial lives or our education or even our ministry. An opportunity we wanted gets closed off, and we feel like our lives are diminished and heaven doesn't care.

And yet . . .

Surely it must be a good thing that God alone has the power to shut in such a way that what is shut cannot be opened. So often a closed door that frustrated me at the time has become the occasion for gratitude later on. I actually find myself saying, "Thank God for closed doors":

- For the girl who rejected me, or else I would not have ended up with my wife
- For the graduate school that turned me down, or I wouldn't have ended up getting to do the work I love to do
- For the writing ventures that got a polite "no thanks," or I never would have learned the need for perseverance and growth
- For the job that was so painfully difficult—because it led to a new determination
- For the promise of early success that did not pan out, because it led to a humbler acceptance of reality
- For the prayer that went unanswered for years, because I learned more on that journey than I ever would have learned through immediate gratification
- For what looked like a great financial opportunity that I missed, because it kept me from getting

involved with an organization that ended up being
fundamentally unhealthy

I thank God for these closed doors. But not for *all* closed
doors. There are many I still don't like and would kick in
if I could. And there are ambiguous doors. Jesus himself,
when speaking about the need for persistence in prayer, said,
"Knock, and the door shall be opened." But he didn't say
which door. He didn't say how loud we should have to knock
or how long we should keep it up. How do I know which
closed doors I should keep knocking at? How do I know
whether I should keep pursuing this job, this girl, this school,
or this dream? How do I know whether I should let it go and
move on?

The good news is that there is a simple two-word answer
to these questions. The bad news is that the two words are
"I don't."

We may never know for sure in this lifetime. God has
greater things in mind for us than "knowing for sure." But
understanding why some doors *shouldn't* be opened can help
us grow in our ability to learn the difference. In this chapter
we'll look at what God might be up to with the closed doors
in our lives.

Knocking at the Wrong Door

Sometimes doors remain closed because we want the wrong
thing.

One day Peter, James, and John are on a mountain with

Jesus, and they see him get radiantly transformed. He is walking around with Moses and Elijah, and Peter says, "Rabbi, it is good for us to be here. Let us put up three shelters—one for you, one for Moses and one for Elijah," as if they're all three on par with each other (Mark 9:5). Peter "did not know what to say, they were so frightened" (verse 6). Apparently the option of silence never occurred to him. Instead, he makes this request, and it's a bad idea, and Jesus says, "No. We have more work to do. That's the wrong request."

Another time, James and John decide they want to upgrade their heavenly seating assignments, so they have their mother kneel before Jesus to ask for seats 1A and 1B in first class. Jesus tells them the Kingdom doesn't really work by getting your mommy to do self-promotion for you. So that's a no.

Another time, they go into a Samaritan village that fails to welcome them—not surprising given ethnic tensions between Samaria and Israel. James and John want to pray fire from heaven to atomize the village.

Jesus says, "Appreciate the gesture, but . . . "

All through the Bible we see closed doors in response to wrong requests. In fact, on four separate occasions, four different people—Moses, Jeremiah, Elijah, and Jonah—all ask God to take their lives. In every case God says, "No, no, no, no." Don't you think when their dark mood was past, they were glad God had said no?

Thank God he sometimes says no.

There is a country song about this by Garth Brooks that hit number one on the charts some time ago called

"Unanswered Prayers." He was at a football game at his old school, and he saw a girl he was nuts about when he was in school. He used to pray God would make that girl his wife. It didn't happen, and now all these years later, he sees her again and wonders, *What was I thinking?*

Under his breath, he whispers, "Thank God! Thank God!" The main line of this song is "Some of God's greatest gifts are unanswered prayers."

I was at my reunion some time ago, and I saw a girl I had been nuts about. Now it was years later, and once more the same prayer got whispered: "Thank God!" I know it got whispered because I heard her whisper it.

Slightly sobering thought: you may be somebody's unanswered prayer.

Doors Close Because There's Something Better

Sometimes a door remains closed because something better lies down the road, only we can't see it.

A young man from an impoverished background dreamed of a better life for himself and his family than the hardscrabble existence he had known growing up. He saved all he could and went deeply into debt to launch a grocery startup. His partner had an alcohol problem, and he ended up so far in the hole that he referred to his financial obligations as "the national debt." He gave up on ever being a successful businessman, and it took him more than a decade to pay off his failed dream.

He went into law, and then politics, and in 1860 Abraham

Lincoln was elected president. He was an avid Shakespeare fan, and his favorite quote came from *Hamlet*: "There is a divinity that shapes our ends, rough-hew them as we may."[1] He came to believe this deeply about his own life, but also about the nation he led. His entire second inaugural address is an amazingly profound reflection on how God was at work in the Civil War in ways more mysterious and profound than any human being could fathom. What a loss it would have been—not just to him but to a whole nation—if the doors of that little grocery he started in New Salem hadn't closed.

It is fundamental to the kind of person God is and to the nature of prayer that God always reserves the right to say no, because he knows what will lead to better outcomes than we do. For every kind of power human beings have access to, we find a way to use it with great destructiveness. It's true for verbal power, financial power, political power, nuclear power.

Imagine that in prayer we had access to supernatural power that would always make things happen the way we wanted them to happen. It would be a disaster. Anybody who thinks that closed doors disprove the efficacy of prayer just has not thought about prayer very deeply.

Prayer is not an incantation. It is a talk with a Person—a very wise Person. So sometimes God will say no, and thank God he does.

Maybe the world's most frequent prayer is "Lord, change her. Change him. Make him be like I want him to be. Make him do what I want him to do."

You may have been praying for that a long time.

It's good to ask God to shape the people in our lives, but often when I pray these prayers my *real* prayer is "God, I don't want to face the reality of my own immaturity, so would you reshape this other person into someone who will accommodate my dysfunction and feed my ego?" And often God has something better in mind. Often that something better is to use that difficult person to change *me*.

Frederick Buechner moved to New York to become a writer, only to find he couldn't write a word. He tried to go into his uncle's advertising business but wasn't tough enough. He tried to join the CIA but didn't have the stomach for it. He fell in love with a girl who did not fall in love with him. He writes, "It all sounds like a kind of inane farce as I set it down here, with every door I tried to open slammed on my foot, and yet I suppose it was also a kind of pilgrim's progress."[2]

It was door closing because he was disappointed in options he wanted. It was progress because it led to him finding, or being found by, God. And in his faith he has written words that have inspired millions of others in their faith. But that door never could have opened if many other doors hadn't closed first.

Doors Close Because I Need to Grow

One day I was praying for an opportunity in leadership, but my mind kept wandering away to a man I was angry with. I remembered there was this really strange prayer in the book of 2 Kings. When some young boys mock Elisha, Elisha actually curses them in the name of the Lord, and a couple of bears arrive to chase those boys away from him. I thought, *I could pray that prayer for this guy.*

I realized my anger was the elephant in the prayer closet, and while I was holding on to it, I was not free to pray with open hands before God. It didn't mean I could make the relationship turn out the way I wanted it to, but there is a big difference between nursing a grudge and surrendering it. I wanted new opportunities for leadership, but what I needed to learn was to grow in the frustration of a difficult relationship where I was.

In the New Testament a man named Simon Magus was so impressed by the spiritual power of the apostle Peter that he offered money to get it. But he didn't really want it to help others; he wanted it to impress them.

His request was denied. Why?

It could be his head wasn't screwed on just right.
It could be, perhaps, that his shoes were too tight.
But I think that the most likely reason of all
May have been that his heart was two sizes too small.[3]

Paul came to God and asked him to remove what Paul called a thorn in the flesh. He asked repeatedly.

All he got in return was a closed door.

But that closed door brought a greater gift than thorn removal. Paul came to understand that grace would come not in removing the thorn but along with the thorn. The thorn, which was painful, would also produce something wonderful in his spirit. The thorn, which somehow was connected with Paul's weakness, would actually enable him to grow in his capacity to be a channel for God's strength. The door to thorn removal was closed so that the door to grace strengthening could be opened.

What are areas where we may need to grow?

- We may need to grow more in generosity and freedom from our need for money, in which case financial doors may close.
- We may need to grow in humility, in which case grandiose wish-fulfillment doors will be closed.
- We may need to grow in our ability to delay gratification, in which case the "Right Now!" door may be closed.
- We may need to grow in our ability to love our enemies, or even our more prickly friends, in which case the "Lord, change him!" door may be closed.

Often, it may be that when the door marked "Go" looks closed, it's because there's a door marked "Grow" that's wide open. I just have to relinquish door sovereignty to God.

Doors Close Because God Has Plans I Don't Know

Israel was the people of God, and they had a dream to be a great nation, but all they experienced was a closed door. They were defeated and cast into exile. Their prayer was to be spared this suffering. What if God had said yes? What if Israel had become a great world power with lots of money and big armies, never had to go into exile, had kept her faith all to herself, and never had prophets who dreamed of another Kingdom, a better Kingdom, a spiritual Kingdom the whole human race could be invited into? When doors of military and political and economic and geographic greatness closed, a small, unseen door to another kind of people on another kind of mission serving another kind of greatness opened and changed the world infinitely more than one more super-power ever could have.

Dietrich Bonhoeffer wanted a quiet life of scholarship and teaching. This door was closed to him. He would labor in an underground seminary and a concentration camp and ultimately sacrifice his life. He could not know that through this he would leave a legacy that would touch hearts around the world for generations.

Years ago Nancy and I moved to Chicago. In many ways this felt like a closed door to Nancy because, for one thing, she's a California native, and Chicago is decidedly not California. More deeply, the alternative we had thought about was a church in California that had offered us both a position, and in Chicago there was no offer on the table for her at all.

She could not know when we made our decision that within a year she'd be on staff at Willow Creek and that she'd become a teaching pastor and that she'd end up leading a ministry that would be the adventure of a lifetime and a chance to shape young leaders who would become lifelong friends and enduring partners in ministry. She didn't know that she'd be building a network of friends and opportunities not just in Chicago but around the world.

Many doors that look large to us are small to God, and many doors that look small to us are very large to him. This is part of the great inversion of the Kingdom: the first will be last, the greatest will be the servant, the lowest will be exalted.

Nicholas Herman was disappointed in his dream of becoming a great soldier. Instead he took an insignificant job as a kitchen worker in a nonmilitary organization. But he made it an experiment to see how much he could depend on God in his work. After he died, a book was compiled called *The Practice of the Presence of God*, which chronicles his life under his monastic name, Brother Lawrence. It has become one of the most widely read books in history. While he was alive, everyone knew who was pope but virtually no one knew Brother Lawrence. Today hardly anyone remembers who was pope then, but the world celebrates the memory of Brother Lawrence.

Even in the cruelty of human evil God can be at work to bring about unexpected good. On her thirteenth birthday, a lonely girl receives a red-and-white checkered autograph book that she uses for a diary. Frustrated by her lack of friends, she decides that her diary will be the one truest friend in whom she will confide the deepest thoughts and feelings that no one else would guess lie in her mind and heart. She lives her life behind closed doors and dies two short years later. The diary of Anne

Frank has become one of the treasured literary gifts of the twentieth century. After the war it was discovered and given to her father—the family's only survivor. Through the humanity and hope of those words in that diary, she has inspired thirty million readers in sixty-seven languages, more than all but a handful of twentieth-century authors. What looked like a small life snuffed out by evil became an inextinguishable light.

Jennifer Dean writes,

> Think of something big. A mountain? A tree? Get a mental picture of something you call big. Now, consider that it is made up of tiny, tiny atoms. Atoms are made up of even tinier neutrons and protons. Neutrons and protons are made up of elements so small that they can't be seen with the strongest microscope.
>
> No such thing as big. Everything we call "big" is just a whole lot of "small."
>
> Small upon small upon small, finally equals big. There is no "big" without lots and lots of small.
>
> Nature as God created it, is the image of the invisible Kingdom of Heaven. . . . In Kingdom living, small matters. Small is the key to big.[4]

In God's Kingdom, small is the new big. In God's Kingdom, the way up is down, and the way to living is dying. Mother Teresa used to advise people not to try to do great things for God, but to do small things with great love.

You and I do not know which doors God will open so that our little lives can have an impact beyond ourselves. We do not know up to the moment of our death—or even beyond—who might be affected by our actions. So we are called to never despair, no matter how small our lives look or how many doors that we desperately wanted to go through appear to have closed. We are invited to live as though God is opening doors that mean that our smallest acts of goodness will somehow, through God's grace, count for all eternity.

God Knows about Closed Doors

God himself knows the agony of more closed doors than any human being ever will. God has given to every human being the key to the door of their own heart, and God himself will not force his way in. "Behold, I stand at the door and knock. . . ." It's not just we who hope God will open a door for us; God hopes we will open a door for him.

So we stand with him in our pain at the closed door.

I got a letter from the father of an eight-year-old daughter who has been diagnosed with a disease that is life threatening and debilitating. He wrote, "Every day I pray for her healing. Every day I pray to understand. Every day I ask God, 'God, would you make me sick instead of my little girl? Let me suffer.' I'm so mad at God. I'm trying to hang on, but I'm so mad. Why is heaven silent on the one prayer I most want answered?"

You have been there, too, or someplace like it. Or you will be sometime. I cannot point you to an explanation that has all the answers because nobody has all the answers. I can only point you to a Person. I can only tell you that at the heart of the gospel is an unanswered prayer. Jesus, kneeling in the garden, prayed, "Father, if it is possible, may this cup, this suffering, this death be taken from me. Yet not my will, but yours, be done."

This is the most desperate prayer ever prayed from the most discerning spirit that ever lived, from the purest heart that ever beat, for deliverance from the most unjust suffering ever known. And all it got was silence. Heaven was not moved. The cup was not taken from him. The request was denied. The door remained closed.

From that unwanted, unmerited suffering came the hope of the world that remade history. Because the ultimate answer to every human anguish, including the anguish of unanswered prayer, is a sin-stained, blood-soaked cross where the Son of God himself suffered. Nobody has all the answers, but I was thinking this week, *What if all those hard prayers were answered yes?*

What if Paul had been healed of his thorn in the flesh and had become even more impressive and traveled even more and learned to boast in his great strength and his great giftedness and turned the movement of the early church into a monument of human greatness?

What if Israel had become "the people of military greatness" or "the people of affluence" instead of "the people of the book"?

Jesus asked in Gethsemane not to be crucified. What if

God had said yes? What if Jesus had been spared that cup? What if there had been no cross, no death, no tomb, no resurrection, no forgiveness of sins, no outpouring of the Holy Spirit, no birth of the church?

I don't know why some prayers get yeses and some prayers get nos. I know the anguish of a no when you want a yes more than you want anything in the world. But I don't know *why*. I only know that in the Cross God's no to his only Son was turned into God's yes to every human being who ever lived.

The Promise beyond All Doors

On the night before he died, Jesus was trying to explain to his disciples how things would look bad for a while, as if heaven had closed its doors, but that they should not give up because it wasn't the end.[5] It's a poignant scene, but at one point John paints a picture of the disciples' thickheadedness that is downright comical:

> Jesus went on to say, "*In a little while* you will see me no more, and then after *a little while* you will see me."
>
> At this, some of his disciples said to one another, "What does he mean by saying, '*In a little while* you will see me no more, and then after *a little while* you will see me . . . '?" They kept asking, "What does he mean by '*a little while*'? We don't understand what he is saying."

Jesus saw that they wanted to ask him about this, so he said to them, "Are you asking one another what I meant when I said, '*In a little while* you will see me no more, and then after *a little while* you will see me'?" (John 16:16-19, emphasis mine)

"Yep," they say. "That's what we're asking."

This is the class for remedial disciples. These are not the Advanced Placement students. In their impatience, they want all doors opened and all questions answered now. To them, "not now" is the same as forever. But to God—and one day to us, in the light of eternity—it is just "a little while." John underlines this so we'll understand what comes next.

Jesus makes them a wonderful promise: "Now is your time of grief, but I will see you again and you will rejoice, and no one will take away your joy. In that day you will no longer ask me anything" (John 16:22-23).

"Joy will win in the end," Jesus says, "and on that day you will ask me no more questions."

What would it mean to have no more questions? Why does Jesus promise this?

The disciples were always pestering Jesus with questions. Have you ever noticed that? Go through the Gospels. All the time it's just "Hey, Jesus! Can I sit at your right hand?" "Hey, Jesus! How many times do I have to forgive this guy?" "Hey, Jesus! Why was this man born blind?" "Hey, Jesus! How come we couldn't cast out this demon?" "Hey, Jesus! What does this parable mean?" "Hey, Jesus! Should we call down fire from heaven to blast the Samaritans?" "Hey, Jesus! Which of us is the greatest?" "Hey, Jesus! What do you mean, 'a little while'?" All the time it's "Hey, Jesus!"

When we had our first child, and she could talk, I learned I was totally unprepared for the constant barrage of questions that came out of that one little mouth. "Why? Why? Why?" They never ended. After a while, I couldn't take it, and my wife, who was home with that child all the time, suffered from it even more. It never stopped. I got so tired of the questions.

One time we were in the car, my wife and I and Laura. She was about two years old, and I got an idea. I decided to turn the tables, so I turned to Laura and began to ask her questions. "Hey, Laura. Why is the grass green? Hey, Laura. Why is the sky blue? Hey, Laura. What makes the sun shine? Hey, Laura. What makes the car go? Hey, Laura. Where do babies come from?" She got this confused, troubled look on her tiny little face, and Nancy got so excited. "Keep going, John. Make her cry. Make her cry."

I was thinking about that and thinking about this passage, and I was wondering, *Did Jesus ever get tired of all the questions?* "Hey, Jesus. Hey, Jesus. Hey, Jesus." Because underneath them all is this really big question: *Why?* Everybody here has that question.

Why? Why does this six-year-old little boy have a brain tumor? Why does a bomb go off in Boston? Why? Hey, Jesus, why is there this disaster in Texas and innocent people lose their lives? Hey, Jesus, why did my child run away? Hey,

Jesus, why did my marriage fall apart? Hey, Jesus, how come I have this crippling depression and I can't make it go away no matter what I do?

Jesus says, "My friends, let me tell you. For a little while you won't see me, and things won't look right. You'll see terrible things in this world. Cancer. Hunger. War. Hatred. Horrible injustice. Bodies being crippled by stuff they should never be crippled by. Betrayal. Abuse. Violation.

"Then, in a little while. . . . It will seem like a long time to you, but in the scale of eternity, it's only a little while. In a little while, in just a little while, in a very little while, I'm coming back, and you will see me again, and I will set it all right, and the world will be reborn, and its birth pangs will be forgotten, and joy will win."

Joy will win.

On this side of the closed door we are filled with questions. Why won't it open? Why can't I have it? Why must I suffer? Someday, somehow, in a way none of us now can understand, we will be as grateful for the closed doors as we are for the open doors now.

Indeed, on that day . . . *on that day*. Not today. Not tomorrow, maybe, but "On that day," Jesus says, "you will ask me no more questions." What a good day that's going to be.

Rudolf Bultmann put it like this: "It is the nature of joy that all questions grow silent and nothing needs explaining."[6]

Then we will see the goodness of God. Then this world will be reborn. Then sin and guilt and pain and suffering and death will be defeated. Then there will be no more questions. If you're tempted to get impatient, and if you wonder when this will ever happen, I will tell you.

In a little while.

In just a little while.

CHAPTER 10

THE DOOR IN THE WALL

Two stories were written in the twentieth century that share the same title: The Door in the Wall.

One of them won the Newbery Medal for children's literature. The ten-year-old son of a medieval knight becomes ill and crippled. He is separated from his parents by a cruel enemy army and cared for by a friar named Brother Luke. He is ashamed and disappointed by his legs—others call him "Robin Crookedshanks." He feels that his life will always be insignificant with him unable to serve and having no chance to show courage or do glorious deeds. But the friar takes him to his monastery, teaches him to read and swim and carve, and teaches him to pray for the faith that a fine and beautiful life still lies before him. "Always remember," the friar says, "thou hast only to follow the wall far enough, and there will be a door in it."

At the end of the story, it is his disability that leads to his opportunity. His crooked legs cause the enemy to underestimate him. The resilient spirit he has grown in response to his challenges keeps him going. He alone finds the door in their fortress wall. Against all odds, he ends up being the rescuer who can steal unsuspected through enemy lines and save the people he loves. It is his faith in the old friar's words that keeps him going.

The other story was written by H. G. Wells, best known for his science fiction works like *The War of the Worlds*. In Wells's story the promise of the door in the wall is a cruel hoax. A man is haunted all his life by the memory of a door that leads to an enchanted garden that contains all he ever longed for. He searches in vain for that door his whole life. At the end of the story his dead body is found—fallen off a construction site behind a wall marked by a door that looks exactly like the one he has been seeking.

We all know about the wall. The wall is our finitude, our problems, our limitations, our disappointments, and ultimately our death. The great question in life is whether the universe has a door in the wall. Maybe not. Maybe life is as Wells pictured it.

But our stories cannot get away from another possibility. At the deepest level, doors are not simply about transitions in our lives, or even opportunities. Doors are about entrance into another reality.

The movie *Monsters, Inc.* is based entirely around doors. In the film, monsters use door portals to enter into children's bedrooms and scare them, since children's fear is the energy that runs the monsters' factory. One door is left "active" and causes a little girl, Boo, to enter the factory. The door opens both ways. The other world invades this one. And in the end the monsters decide to make children laugh rather than scream, because joy turns out to be stronger than fear.

The Bible tells the strange stories of men and women who believe there is another world; that the garden we long for really does exist; that the enemies, suffering and death, will not be allowed to have the last word; that we shall see another world, or see this world put to rights. This belief keeps them—and us—going in the midst of suffering and disappointment: "Faith is confidence in what we hope for and assurance about what we do not see. This is what the ancients were commended for" (Hebrews 11:1-2). And in an ancient world where the gods were often frightening and monstrous, the message arose of one God who said to his friend Abraham, "Oh, the places you'll go," and told him to name his son Isaac "Laughter," because he decided that joy was stronger than fear.

I believe there is a door. I believe it because life itself comes to us as a gift. It is an "opened" door because God is the one who opens it. I cannot force it. This is one of the great laws of the universe: "Life so often releases its gifts only if we do not try hard for them. I am thinking of such things as making friends or getting to sleep or becoming an original thinker or making a good impression in a job interview or becoming happy in life. Try too hard at any of these things and we defeat ourselves. Faith in God is itself much more gift and discovery than deliberate achievement."[1]

"Always remember, thou hast only to follow the wall far enough, and there will be a door in it."

But it is hard for us to remember. We have (God knows) "little strength." Our legs are crooked and easily wearied.

So here, at the end of our exploration of doors, is help to keep us searching for the door when the wall seems insurmountable. We will look at the main reasons why human beings are tempted to give up the search. And we'll remember not to quit searching.

"I'm Not Strong Enough"

Sometimes I'm tempted to give up looking for divine opportunities to partner with God when I am overwhelmed by a sense of my own inadequacy. For example, I try to meditate on a verse about love in the Bible ("It does not envy, it does not boast, it is not proud," 1 Corinthians 13:4). My very next thought is how I might teach others about that verse with great effectiveness, and my next thought is how impressed people will be with my teaching and how I can use that verse on love to become a great success.

I think about another door mentioned in Scripture. God spoke to Cain when Cain was tempted by envy and hate: "Why are you angry, and why has your countenance fallen? If you do well, will you not be accepted? And if you do not do well, sin is lurking at the door; its desire is for you, but you must master it" (Genesis 4:6-7, NRSV).

The "door" here is what might be called a "door of temptation." In any moment when I'm tempted, God promises to be present and make a way of escape possible. Sometimes I remember this and close the door on temptation. Sometimes I don't.

I got a phone call from a really cranky neighbor. Ever had one of those? What she said felt unfair and scathing and judgmental. I always have to be careful with that sort of thing because I'm a pastor, and you never know when someone you talk to in one context will end up at your church. But still . . . it just made me mad.

I could feel the temperature rising inside me. Then I remembered that Jesus said, "Love your neighbor" (Matthew 22:39). I said, "All right, Jesus. This neighbor needs to experience patience and love. I will have Nancy call her up."

I talked to a man waiting my table at a restaurant who is working two minimum-wage jobs. Not one, but *two* minimum-wage jobs, just to make ends meet and to support his mom. I wasn't going to do anything particularly generous. Then I remembered Jesus said, "Do not store up for yourselves treasures on earth. . . . But store up for yourselves treasures in heaven" (Matthew 6:19-20). This man's need became an open door for a small gesture, for a quick prayer.

Every moment (even at the oddest times) the door to heaven is open. I was driving in bumper-to-bumper freeway traffic when I was in a hurry. (The more hurried you are, the slower the traffic is.) To make things worse, a man drove past everybody on the left-hand shoulder where you're not supposed to. It's not a lane. It's the shoulder. It was as if he owned the whole road, and then he wanted to get in front of me to get to the exit ramp.

To make it worse, I looked at him. I didn't want to, but I knew it wasn't right to ignore him. He looked at me and tapped his watch as if I were wasting his time. And Jesus had words for this circumstance too: "Get thee behind me, Satan."

Jesus has words for every occasion. That's the wonderful thing about him.

Sometimes I remember them and do them. But often I don't. I yell at my family. I put myself first. I value people because they're useful to me. I work to impress people I find impressive. I make myself the hero of my stories. I covet. I envy.

And then I look in the mirror, and I'm ready to give up on myself.

I was standing in line at the grocery store and noticed a woman ahead of me who was dressed in such a way that I could get a little surge of sexual gratification by simply watching her and dwelling on the sight. I had always thought that simply by becoming a pastor, I would automatically mature beyond such experiences, but so far that hormonal bypass hasn't kicked in yet.

And then a thought occurred to me, as if out of nowhere: *What would I do right now if my friend Dallas Willard were standing in line with me?* Dallas was an enormously helpful spiritual influence on me, as on so many others. He had died recently, and I found myself thinking of him often. And more than most people I know, he had mastered seeing the beauty in all people but in a way that was largely liberated from wrongful or objectifying desire.

I knew in that moment that if I were standing with Dallas, I would not be staring at that woman. And I knew that while at one level I would like momentary gratification, at a deeper level, in my better self, I would like to live more the way that Dallas lived. I would like to not repress illicit desire but be free of it.

And I remembered that, far more important than Dallas, Jesus is in some sense standing with me. I remembered that this is what Dallas saw and taught and lived, and it's why I loved him and was so drawn to him. I realized when I looked at Dallas closely, his is the best way to live.

And I stopped looking. The door closed.

"Sin is lurking at the door," Cain is told, "but you must master it." How is that done? Not, oddly enough, by force. At this door, the door of the mind, mastery comes through surrender. If I use willpower to try to make myself not envy, or compare, or dislike, it does little good. But there is another way.

In the middle of a wonderful passage to the Philippians where Paul writes about having minds that are liberated from anxiety and occupied with joy and whatever is true and honorable and just and worthy of praise, he makes this wonderful promise: "And the peace of God, which transcends all understanding, will guard your hearts and your minds in Christ Jesus" (Philippians 4:7).

I do not have to stand guard at this door alone. God will help me with it if I ask.

In the same letter, Paul makes another wonderful statement. He says that he himself has not arrived yet. He does one thing: "Forgetting what is behind and straining toward what is ahead, I press on toward the goal" (Philippians 3:13-14).

"Forgetting what is behind." One of the great tasks of the spiritual life is learning what to remember and what to forget. I am to forget "what is behind." My guilt, my inadequacy, my weakness, my regrets. "I know you have little strength," God says.

I am to remember to press on. "Always remember, thou hast only to follow the wall far enough, and there will be a door."

"God Is Not Good Enough"

The next reason I'm tempted to give up looking for the door is I'm afraid God will give up on me. This is the rationale of the man who wasted his talent in Jesus' parable. The man says to his master, "I knew that you are a hard man" (Matthew 25:24).

I forget the price God has paid to open the door of heaven to me.

The first year of our marriage my wife and I traveled to Sweden and learned the story of my grandfather's family that, in true Swedish fashion, my grandfather never told us.

We went to the old parish church that the Ortberg family had attended a century ago, and reading through the records, we pieced together the story. When my grandfather was nine years old, his mother died. The means of her death was the ingestion of sulfur, which means either she was attempting suicide or trying to abort a child. Either way, it was not tolerable to the church. When she died, they would not bury her in the church graveyard. Somewhere outside the little gated graveyard of that church, my great-grandmother was buried, and her nine-year-old boy could not know the place, could not visit the body of his mother. She was outside the gate.

He left Sweden and came to the States, met his wife, and raised his family here, and I'm grateful he did because otherwise my father, and then I, would never have been born. He worked, among other jobs, as janitor at the high school my dad attended. He was an old man when I knew him—ninety-three when he died—and in some ways I suppose he had been outside looking in his whole life.

In many ways, that's all of us. The Bible begins with a picture of life with no doors, where a man and a woman know intimacy with God and with each other without shame and without death. But we don't live there anymore. In response to sin, the Bible describes the first door: "[God] drove out the man; and at the east of the garden of Eden he placed the cherubim, and a sword flaming and turning to guard the way to the tree of life" (Genesis 3:24, NRSV). The first door is a closed door. We are outside the gate.

The cherubim guarding the door of Eden is a little picture of the Temple, where cherubim sat on the Ark of the Covenant guarding the Holy of Holies. That was the most sacred part of the Temple, accessible only to one person on one day of the year.

It's a picture of the search we all are on for the door we cannot find. We are all outside the gate. But God doesn't want anyone left outside. God is always trying to bring prodigals home. The door to the Father's house is always left open.

And somehow, Jesus took on our "outsideness." In fact, in the book of Hebrews it says that Jesus suffered "outside the city gate" to make people holy (13:12).

When Jesus died, we're told the veil that guarded the holiest place was torn in two. The presence of God was now, through Jesus, available to anyone who wants it. This is the ultimate door, the doorway to heaven, the door we have been searching for since Eden, the door before which we were all hopeless, outside looking in.

Sin is a room with no door. There is a reason why Jean-Paul Sartre, who famously said that "hell is other people," titled his portrait of hell "No Exit."

But there is always a door.

Who left the door open?

> Most assuredly, I say to you, I am the door of the
> sheep. . . . I am the door. If anyone enters by Me,
> he will be saved, and will go in and out and find
> pasture. The thief does not come except to steal, and
> to kill, and to destroy. I have come that they may
> have life, and that they may have it more abundantly.
> (John 10:7, 9-10, NKJV)

Jesus himself is the door. No other human being has ever said this about themselves—not Buddha, not Confucius, not Muhammad; not Caesar or Napoleon or Big Bird. Jesus said it. Through Jesus—the door, the way, the portal—up there has come down here.

"See, I have placed before you an open door."

Jesus became an outsider so we could be invited in. Jesus left his home so that we could come home. When the disciple John was a young man, he heard his friend Jesus say, "I am the door." When John was an old man, he was given one more great vision of his friend: "After this I looked, and there before me was a door standing open in heaven" (Revelation 4:1). Jesus left the door open.

All of us have been searching for a door that lies beyond our grasp, and we often look for it in wrong ways. There is a quote sometimes credited to G. K. Chesterton but whose real source is unknown: "Every time a man knocks at the door of a brothel, he is really searching for God."

A brothel is a scandalous place. But Jesus scandalized people by welcoming scandalous women into the circle of his redeeming love. When Jesus knocked on the door of a brothel, it wasn't man searching for God. It was God searching for man.

God is good enough. God is *better* than good enough. God's goodness is reason enough to keep following the wall until we find the door.

"The World Is Not Safe Enough"

We go through open doors for freedom and adventure and life; but we avoid them when we are afraid. We come in behind doors for safety and rest. Doors are the most important part of the walls around a city or the walls of a house. They are necessary but also vulnerable and therefore guarded.

Because of this, the most important words in Israel's life were door words. They come from Deuteronomy 6:4-5: "Hear, O Israel: The LORD our God, the LORD is one. Love the LORD your God with all your heart and with all your soul and with all your strength." These words were called the *Shema*, from the first Hebrew word, which means "hear."

The Israelites were to remember and talk about these words when they went in and when they went out. They were to write them on the doorposts of their houses and on their gates. They would come to be called *mezuzahs*, handwritten, tightly rolled parchment scrolls enclosed in small containers and placed on the door. Twenty-two lines containing the first two paragraphs of the Shema. On the back of the parchment would be inscribed the single word: *Shaddai*—"Almighty."

The three consonants in this word were thought to be an acronym for "Guardian of the Doors of Israel."

It was to be a reminder that God was watching over them at all times. In Hebrew, the phrase "when you go in and when you go out" was an all-inclusive description of the totality of a person's life, similar to how we might tell someone, "Call me night or day" when we want them to know we are available at any moment.

This is an important point, because I often think that what I need in order to be free of anxiety is a guaranteed outcome. But I'm wrong. It's not what's on the other side of the door that gives me confidence to go through; it's the one who goes with me.

For I'll tell you another secret about open doors. What we want most is not what lies behind the door. What we want most is the one who opens it. Always, when we go through the opened door, we go with him. He meets human beings at the threshold. The magic of the open door is not the new circumstances or job or location or accomplishment. It's actually being with him that turns where we are into Wonderland.

There is a Talmudic story that a king once sent a pearl to the era's most famous rabbi, Rav. Rav sent back a simple mezuzah. The king was furious at the great discrepancy in value. Rav explained, "The gift you sent me is so valuable that it will have to be guarded, whereas the gift I sent you will guard you." He quoted Proverbs 6:22: "When you walk it will lead you; when you lie down it will watch over you."[2]

Israel would remember that it was the blood of a sacrificial lamb spread on their doors that protected them from judgment and death during the great days of the Exodus. The very act of walking through a door, from the safety of home into a world of dangers, became a sacred reminder of God's loving protection.

God's presence and power make us safer than any merely human-powered protection ever could. This promise is behind one of the great pictures of the Old Testament:

> Lift up your heads, you gates;
>> be lifted up, you ancient doors,
>>> that the King of glory may come in.
> Who is this King of glory?
>> The Lord strong and mighty,
>>> the Lord mighty in battle. (Psalm 24:7-8)

Because doors were the most vulnerable part of ancient city walls, they were not to be opened easily. Once open, any enemy could rush in and overwhelm the city. But in this case they were to be opened, for in this case it was safety that was coming into the city.

From a human perspective, the great enemy is Death, our final, fearsome foe. In the ancient world, stoicism rather than hope when facing death was regarded as the most admirable and fitting virtue. The man (always a man, in the ancient world) who had mastered his inner fears and anxieties was said to be a "Conqueror."

Paul chose his words carefully: "Who shall separate us

from the love of Christ? Shall trouble or hardship or persecution or famine or nakedness or danger or sword? . . . No, in all these things we are more than conquerors through him who loved us" (Romans 8:35, 37). "More than conquerors" is more than a phrase. It's a claim. It's a promise. The ultimate battle is not me fighting my fears of undefeatable doom. It is Christ defeating doom.

The wall is not all. Only keep following. There will be a door. You'll recognize it by the sign: "More than Conquerors."

"The Way Isn't Clear Enough"

"Knock, and it will be opened to you," Jesus said.

But he didn't say how long we'd have to knock. He didn't tell us how to infallibly choose the right door. He didn't give us a formula to know which option to pick. Moses kept praying through forty years of wilderness travel and never got into the Promised Land. Paul kept asking for the thorn in his flesh to be removed, and it never was. I may be tempted to give up looking for the door because I don't know where to look.

There's an old saying for travelers. A car's headlights only shine for fifteen feet, but that fifteen feet will get you all the way home. God knows just how much clarity will be good for us—not too much, and not too little. We don't follow clarity. We follow *God*.

Bob Goff writes about how he desperately wanted to become a lawyer so that he could make an impact on the world in the area of justice. He knew the law school he wanted to attend. The only problem was they didn't admit him.

So he went to the dean's office, introduced himself, explained his situation, and described how badly he wanted to attend this school even though they had rejected him.

"I understand," said the dean. "Have a nice day."

Bob decided to keep knocking. "You have the power to change my life," Bob said. "All you have to say to me is 'Go buy your books,' and I could be a student in your school."

The dean smiled. "Have a nice day."

Bob decided to camp in the dean's office. There were five days before school started. When the dean would arrive in the morning, there would be Bob. "Four words. 'Go buy your books.' Change my life."

Smile. "Have a nice day."

Bob wouldn't go away. He came to know the dean's routine—when he arrived, when he went home, when he took a break for lunch, when he went to the gym. Every time he saw him, he'd remind him: "Four words. Change my life."

The day law school started, Bob knew it was going to be his day. He saw the dean a dozen times that day. Each time the same message. "Just tell me to buy my books."

"Have a nice day."

Then came day two of law school. Bob was already starting to fall behind, and he hadn't even gotten in. By day five Bob was beginning to worry. Late in the afternoon he heard footsteps. By now he knew both the dean's footsteps and his schedule by heart. The dean was not supposed to be out of his office at this time.

He looked Bob in the eye, gave him a wink, and told him the four words that changed his life: "Go buy your books."

Bob bought the books.

He went on to serve God in remarkable ways, including international diplomacy and teaching at law school. But here's what he wrote about getting in:

> I once heard somebody say that God had closed a door on an opportunity they had hoped for. But I've always wondered if, when we want to do something that we know is right and good, God places that desire deep in our hearts because He wants it for us and it honors Him. Maybe there are times when we think a door has been closed and, instead of misinterpreting the circumstances, God wants us to kick it down. Or perhaps just sit outside of it long enough until somebody tells us we can come in.[3]

Imagine if he'd left the dean's office on day four. Always remember to keep following the wall. Just don't give up.

Ella Fitzgerald was singing "Mack the Knife" to a crowd in Berlin. It was her first time singing the song, and partway through she forgot the lyrics. Most people would consider quitting at that point. Ella decided to keep going. She made up words as she went along, and they rhymed and fit the music and proved such a tour de force that she ended up winning a Grammy for it.

Mary Cahill was a suburban mom. Challenged to write about what she knew, she joked that she'd have to call her book *Carpool.* Challenged again, she sat down and wrote a novel: *Carpool: A Novel of Suburban Frustration.* Nine rejections later she sold it to Random House. It became a Literary Guild selection, and Viacom bought the movie rights.

Often the open and closed doors of our lives are a mystery to us. Paul wanted to carry out his ministry in Asia but was "forbidden by the Holy Spirit" (Acts 16:6, NRSV). (What might that have been like?) Then he wanted to go to some place called Bithynia, "but the Spirit of Jesus would not allow them to" (verse 7). All this with no explanation. Until Paul got a vision: a man in Macedonia pleading with him and saying, "Come over to Macedonia and help us" (verse 9).

And so he did.

And so the word of Jesus came to Europe. Through an open door. But it started with an unexplained closed door first.

Paul began to preach the gospel, but it got him into trouble with people who stood to lose a considerable amount of money, so Paul and Silas were thrown in jail. That night there was an earthquake that shook the prison, and "immediately all the doors were opened" (Acts 16:26, NRSV). If I had been Paul, I'm quite certain I would have taken them as God-opened doors and gone through them at once. But Paul did not go through those doors. He immediately assured the jailer, "Don't harm yourself! We are all here!" (verse 28), because if the jailer lost the prisoners, his own life would be forfeit. And that opened a door in the hearts of the jailer and his family to the gospel that would never have opened otherwise.

What a remarkable life. When doors appeared to be closed to Paul, he waited on greater ones. When doors appeared to be open to his freedom, he chose not to go through them so that a greater door might be honored.

God often gives us just enough clarity to take the next step in following him. In Acts 12 Peter was arrested and condemned to die. The church, we're told, prayed fervently to God for him. That very night an angel was sent to Peter and led him out of his chains. They "came before the iron gate leading into the city. It opened for them of its own accord" (verse 10, NRSV). What wonderful language! What a remarkable experience for a gate to have its own will for a moment.

Peter went to the home where all the disciples were gathered, praying for him. He knocked at the gate, and a woman named Rhoda answered. "On recognizing Peter's voice, she was so overjoyed that, instead of opening the gate, she ran in and announced that Peter was standing at the gate" (Acts 12:14, NRSV). (Rhoda was apparently more feeler than thinker.) The rest of the story is too rich not to quote:

> They said to her, "You are out of your mind!" But she insisted that it was so. They said, "It is his angel." Meanwhile Peter continued knocking; and

when they opened the gate, they saw him and were amazed. (Acts 12:15-16, nrsv)

God is the God of the open door.

Meanwhile, the centuries come and go. Generations of human beings find, or fail to find, the open doors God places before them.

And now it is your day. Now it is your door.

Who knows what lies before you this day? What person might need your encouragement? What insight might you have or problem might you solve or learning might you discover or piece of service might you offer? You might help to further the cause of justice, to stop some act of oppression, to relieve someone's burden, to enhance someone's dignity.

You might do something eternal.

The Bible begins with a door that is closed, the door to Eden that we search for all our lives. At the end, the Bible pictures life as God redeems it. It pictures a city of surpassing brilliance and radiant joy and moral beauty and knowing beyond shame. It will be a place of endless opportunity before a loving God, where those who have been faithful in even a little here on earth will be placed in charge of whole cities.

And one last thing. Always, in the ancient world, there were walls with gates, and the gates needed to be guarded, and the gates needed to be closed, because danger and death were never far away.

In the city that is to come, we're told, there will be twelve gates, each made of a single pearl. That's where the expression "pearly gates" comes from, although the Bible is talking about something no oyster can produce.

The number twelve would remind each reader of how many disciples there were, which in turn reminded people of how many tribes there were in Israel, which in turn meant to people that there's room for everybody.

You have a gate.

"The nations will walk by its light, and the kings of the earth will bring their glory into it. Its gates will never be shut by day—and there will be no night there" (Revelation 21:24-25, NRSV).

The final door is an open door.

It's still open.

"Always remember, thou hast only to follow the wall far enough."

Afterword

I LEARNED THE SECRET of the open door from a red-haired, bony-fingered, middle-aged Greek professor named Gerald Hawthorne.

I did not know when I signed up to take a Greek class in college that it was a door into a world of ideas that would change my life and shape my calling. I did not know that it would lead to a circle of friends who remain with me to this day, or to a mentor who would challenge and direct my sense of vocation. I did not know that it would lead to the woman I would marry or the job I would take or the person I would become. All I knew then was that my friend Kevin said he'd heard Dr. Hawthorne was a teacher not to be missed and that taking ancient Greek sounded easier than taking Spanish because no one can tell if you mispronounce it.

We never know what the doors we walk through will lead to. Sometimes we don't even know a door is there. Sometimes the door comes as pure gift.

You wouldn't think a Greek class at eight o'clock in the morning three times a week would be a riveting experience. But you'd be wrong. No one came late—not because we'd get penalized, but because Dr. Hawthorne would begin the class with five minutes of inspirational thoughts rooted in the New Testament that could change your life.

And one day, those five minutes were devoted to the secret of the open door.

> To the angel of the church in Philadelphia write:
> These are the words of him who is holy and true,
> who holds the key of David. What he opens no
> one can shut, and what he shuts no one can open.
> I know your deeds. See, I have placed before you an
> open door that no one can shut. I know that you
> have little strength, yet you have kept my word and
> have not denied my name. (Revelation 3:7-8)

He began his remarks with a little grammar lesson. Dr. Hawthorne had a passion for grammar. He loved the rationality and order of language. He would often declare, when we complained about the difficulty of learning Greek, that there was no such thing as an irregular Greek verb. I didn't even know what an irregular verb was—it sounded to me like a verb with a digestive problem. But Jerry loved to poke around the nuances of language to find richness beneath the surface.

In this passage, he began by noting a feature of the perfect tense in Greek. It describes a past act that is over and done with but whose effects continue to the present. One sees it beautifully illustrated in 1 Corinthians 15:3-5, where it is surrounded by a whole series of aorist tense verbs that describe simple past actions:

Christ died;

Christ was buried;

Christ was seen by Peter;

Christ appeared to the Twelve—and so on.

But right in the middle of all these simple past tenses, the perfect tense is used to describe the resurrection of Christ—he was raised from the dead and is still the resurrected one. The effect of the Resurrection in the past is that Christ is alive now.

This is the tense used here in Revelation 3:8—the door was opened, and it stands open now.

There is a door that is open to you. In the mystery of divine providence it may have been opened long ago, but it remains open now. The result is that this moment is alive with opportunity. This is a staggering truth about life that we are mostly blind to.

However, Jerry said, there is an even more exciting teaching in this passage.

The adjective is not only a perfect participle but a perfect *passive* participle—not simply an "open door," but an "*opened* door." "Did you catch that?" he would ask excitedly. "Can you hear the difference?"

As we have seen, many of the New Testament writers, with their devout Jewish backgrounds, avoided using the sacred name "God" lest they failed to use it reverently. This tendency is sometimes called "the divine passive," and the passive structure was often used to refer to the activity of God without having to make use of the word *God*.

So this door that the living Lord of the church is talking about here is not merely an open door, such as might be left unintentionally open by a careless boy, but a divinely opened door, a door intentionally, thoughtfully, purposefully, deliberately opened by God himself in front of us.

These, then, Jerry said, are the marvelous ideas that swirl around this powerful image of the door. The Lord Jesus stands beside us and calls us to realize something stupendous—"Look, I have given you a door flung wide open by God. There it is. It is my gift to you, and it is right in front of you!" A door!

This is the door, to revisit the words of the teacher I love, that is symbolic "of boundless opportunities! Of unlimited chances to do something worthwhile; of grand openings into new and unknown adventures of significant living; of heretofore unimagined chances to do good, to make our lives count for eternity."[1]

Then Jerry spoke of his own life as a series of opened doors.

He had the opportunity to attend a college where he felt far less gifted than other students. He would often say that he was, like Winnie the Pooh, a bear of very little brain. Anytime a student of his did anything outstanding, he would say, "It's one more example of a student exceeding his teacher." He would say this even though he was the most beloved teacher at Wheaton College for four decades, even though his commentary on Philippians is one of the best ever written.

He was intimidated about even attending college because he was afraid he was not bright enough. But then, he said, his mind returned to this text. There he noted that Christ not only said, "Look, I have given you a God-opened door!" but he also said, "Look! I know your strength is small!"

What came to him in those words was "Look! I don't give you opened doors without supplying you with the courage and the strength and the power to go through them. When you have used up your little strength, draw on mine. So stop worrying about your ability. Stop making weakness an excuse for drawing back and turning away from this opportunity. Remember, it is the weak who can become strong. Remember that my strength is made perfect in your weakness!"

When Jerry graduated, he was offered the chance to teach Greek at Wheaton. Again, he was overwhelmed by his own sense of inadequacy, but as he prayed, he sensed the risen Lord saying, "Look! I have given you this divinely opened door, and yes, I know that you have but little strength. Remember, however, that all power has been given to me. So don't turn away from this opportunity!"

John Masefield's touchingly awkward poem of a lonely, fearful young man in a far country also came to mind:

> I have seen flowers come in stony places;
> And kindness done by men with ugly faces;
> And the gold cup won by the worst horse at the races;
> So I trust, too.

Like Masefield's young man, Jerry said, he trustingly put his hand into the hand of the Lord and stepped through the door that God had opened for him and into the most "joyous, challenging, exhilarating occupation anyone could have imagined."

(You might not think anyone would describe teaching ancient Greek with these words. But you'd be wrong. God's got a door with your name on it.)

Then Jerry said, "If there is any lesson from all these experiences of life, many of which have made me afraid—if there is any lesson I'd like to share with you today, irrespective of your age, or the condition of your health, it is this: our God is the God of the open door, the door of boundless opportunities that keep opening to us as long as we live, all the way from doing something that may seem far too big for us, to doing some little act of kindness (which in reality is a very big act indeed in our increasingly harsh, uncaring, unfeeling world!)."

Open doors are never simply about us. Because Dr. Hawthorne went through these doors, the lives of hundreds of students were changed, including mine. He was the teacher and mentor of that circle of friends I mentioned at the beginning of this chapter. He challenged us, taught us, believed in us, prodded us. When I was nearing the end of my college days, he pulled me aside: "John, I think you ought to go to California, and I think you ought to study at Fuller Seminary." I had lived in Illinois my whole life. I did not really want to go to California. I thought the people who lived in California were flaky, and I would miss my family.

I applied to Fuller for a program to get a degree in clinical psychology as well as a divinity degree. Dr. Hawthorne said, "If you get in, I think you ought to take it as a door God has opened for you, and I think you should be willing to leave where you feel comfortable and secure and go someplace where you can learn and grow and be stretched. Then I think you should take all you can learn about psychology and theology and see if you can make your life an adventure in serving God."

So I went.

I had no idea what it would mean. I had no idea I would turn out to be a lousy therapist, that when clients came to see me, they would actually end up more emotionally immature than they had been before they saw me. But I would never have known that if I hadn't gone through the door. How glad I was to learn it quickly, not after thirty or forty years of therapeutic malpractice.

At that same time, I met a pastor named John F. Anderson ("The 'F' is for Frederick," he would always say modestly, "as in Frederick the Great"). John invited me to work at the church he led, First Baptist Church at La Crescenta, just a few hours a week at the beginning. I had no idea I was meeting with somebody who would believe in me so much that he would change my life. I had no idea, when I walked through the door of that church for the first time, that I was entering into a vocation and not just a building.

He was another great door opener in my life. He and his wife, Barb, opened their home to me, for friendship is an open door. From John I learned the great lesson that ministry should be joy. Once when he and I were in downtown Los Angeles, he walked into the middle of a park and announced with great dignity that he was so pleased so many people had come to the park, and that I, his young associate, would be delivering a fiery message—which I then did, yelling in my best Baptist style. I can remember many times in their home that were so funny we would literally lie on the living room carpet and laugh.

John asked me to preach, and early on one time when I got up to preach, about five minutes into the sermon, I fainted. We had a marble platform, and I just went down. *Boom!* I told John afterward, "I'm so sorry," especially because it was a Baptist church, not a charismatic church where you get credit for going down while you're preaching. "I will understand if you don't ever have me preach again." He said, "Don't be ridiculous," and he had me preach again.

I began speaking when I was very young, and I loved it, although it also terrified me. Fainting while I was preaching made me wonder whether this door would be closed to me.

The very next time I preached, I fainted again. I was sure *that* was the end, and John said, "No, it's not the end. I'm going to have you preach again next week. I will have you preach until you quit fainting or it kills you." And he did. I noticed he had the platform carpeted—nice, thick, soft, shag carpet. But I kept preaching.

I got a letter from that church not long ago, asking if I would preach for their seventy-fifth anniversary. John has long since retired, and the current pastor wrote, "The people here still remember you," which was flattering, until he said, "as the fainting pastor. They still remember you." So I've decided to go back there and preach for their seventy-fifth anniversary. And I've decided to faint again just for old time's sake. I hope they still have the shag carpet.

I never knew that through this move, through that church, I would meet Nancy. I had always thought that if I ever did get married, it would be to a Midwestern girl. I'd settle in the Midwest. But Nancy—a California girl—married me, and we had California children, and we have a California dog, and we get to serve at a California church. I have to tell you, I am grateful beyond words for this life. I'm grateful beyond words for how God is with me, has been with me so many times, even though I fail and am so inadequate.

When Dr. Hawthorne retired, the college gave a banquet in his honor. We, his students, talked about how some of the best moments in life were the times when we skipped chapel (the administration was not thrilled by this) to talk and pray and laugh and learn with Jerry, because so many doors opened to our minds and hearts in those moments.

"I do not want to retire," Jerry said, "in the sense of stepping back from any God-opened door before me, saying 'Let me rest now, leave me alone, I've done my job, I've had enough. Count me out. Give me the hammock.'"

He became the great encourager of the entire school, from student to faculty to administration. He would cheer on former students in their work. He taught in churches.

He took on another mammoth undertaking: to write a

commentary on the book of Colossians. This time, though, a door slowly began to close. His memory began to betray him. We would get together for summit breakfasts, as we had in the old days, but he would forget punch lines and names. He would sometimes resort to simply making a snarling sound when words eluded him. Yet his pain at forgetting could not defeat his desire to be present with those he loved.

You might think that being an open-door kind of person is reserved for people with naturally resilient temperaments or people with genetically high levels of confidence and optimism. But you'd be wrong. Jerry was one of those people who wrestled with self-doubt and anxiety his whole life. But that, too, was part of his gift. There was a kind of awareness of brokenness in him that meant people found him a refuge. People shared secrets and pain with him that they never would have shared with a self-confident, never-failed kind of person.

It's just that Jerry was so habitually committed to walking through open doors he could never break himself of that habit.

You might think it safer to avoid the door, to stay where you are. Ironically, we sometimes shy away from life's open doors because we feel weak or tired. We're afraid one more door will wear us out. But retreating from doors drains the human spirit far more than charging through them does. Jerry used to cite an old rabbinic legend that captures this:

From the mint two bright, new pennies came,
The value and beauty of both the same;

One slipped from the hand and fell to the ground,
Then rolled out of sight and could not be found.

The other was passed by many a hand,
Through many a change in many a land;
For temple dues paid, now used in the mart,
Now bestowed on the poor by a pitying heart.
At length it so happened, as years went round,
That the long lost, unused coin was found.
Filthy and black, its inscription destroyed,
Through rusting peacefully unemployed.

Whilst the well-worked coin was bright and clear
Through active service year after year;
For the brightest are those who live for duty—
Rust, more than rubbing, will tarnish beauty.[2]

He once put it like this: "So old though I am, and often feeling my age, I do not want to shut my eyes to any door that God has opened for me at the beginning of each new day. I do not want to turn away from stepping through it because I am too fearful or too weary, for there is still much good that needs to be done. I ask you to join me in this life-long challenge of stepping through the God-opened doors of opportunity that our Lord Jesus Christ gives to us as long as we have life and breath!"

On the weekend of Wheaton's 150th anniversary I flew back out to Illinois, and a group of us got together with Jerry for breakfast one more time. He prayed, by first name and last, for each of us around the table, as if it were thirty-five years ago. That was the last time I saw him.

We all gathered that next August for his memorial service. The family had to borrow a larger church for it—too many people gathered to fit in the church Jerry had always attended. Beyond that, hundreds of people went to an online site to write how much their lives had been changed by this one man.

At that memorial, his son Steve gave us the notes for Jerry's open-door thoughts. He also showed me in one of Jerry's old Greek New Testaments the laboriously printed reminder where Jerry would pray for me, my wife, and each of our three children by name, along with countless other students and their families.

He never stopped going through open doors. He just finally went through a door where we could not follow. Yet.

Doors will open. The question is, Will I see? Will I respond?

One of Jerry's old students, David Church, went on to become a teacher like Jerry. He wrote a poem around these thoughts called "The Risk of the Open Door":

The fear of moving through
That vortex between
Universes, which (even
If the first could be revisited)
Would not be
As it was: safe, charming.
   Yet the door has been opened

And I am before it.
What strange wind brushes my damp brow?
If I turn back
To the charming safety
Of these familiar spaces,
That rectangle of shifting shadows
On the floor of my universe,
Sometimes dark, sometimes golden,
Sometimes hot white, will burn
In me like an unanswered question,
Like a friendship neglected,
Like a love missed.
Heart pounding. God
Help me, I
Go.

For we follow the Lord of the Open Door.

Jesus was always ready to go through whatever open door his Father set before him.

At whatever cost. And the cost was great.

In the end, they hung him on a cross, and cut his body down, and laid it in a tomb, and sealed it with a stone. And for two days he lay there. For two days the world was cold and closed and empty.

But on the third day, the Father said to the Son: "See, I have placed before you an open door."

And he came through to the other side.

That door is still open.

Acknowledgments

BOOKS, LIKE LIVES, are also the products of many open doors. This is the first book I have done with the Tyndale team, and I am most grateful for the partnership and the joy of working together. Ron Beers has been an unending source of encouragement and ideas and enthusiasm. Carol Traver brings more energy and twisted (in the best sense of the word) wit than any writer has a right to expect. Jonathan Schindler added wonderful contributions to the thoughts expressed as well as how they could be best articulated. Curtis and Sealy Yates have been joy-filled advocates and cheerleaders. Brad Wright and the SoulPulse gang have been a great source of ideas and direction and social science expertise. I have been especially grateful during the writing of this book for the clinical research to which I was introduced at Fuller Theological Seminary by folks like Neil Warren and Arch Hart and Newt Malony and Richard Gorsuch.

I am grateful to the elders and congregation of Menlo Park Presbyterian Church for giving me time and space to write. Linda Barker, with whom I work there, brings a level of order and joy to daily life without which a task like this would be impossible.

I am grateful for Nancy, who has never to my knowledge turned down an open door and has forced her way past more than her share of apparently closed ones, because I cannot imagine a better human being with whom to walk toward the divine possibilities of life.

For Gerald P. Hawthorne, who instructed so many students at Wheaton College over the decades in New Testament Greek and friendship and laughter and love and faith, there are not enough words.

Notes

CHAPTER 1: ALL THE PLACES TO GO . . . HOW WILL YOU KNOW?

1. These six-word memoirs are from *Not Quite What I Was Planning: Six-Word Memoirs by Writers Famous and Obscure*, eds. Rachel Fershleiser and Larry Smith (New York: HarperCollins, 2008).

2. Gerald Hawthorne, *Colossians* (self-published commentary, 2010).

3. Viktor E. Frankl, *Man's Search for Meaning* (Boston: Beacon Press, 2006), 66.

4. Sheena Iyengar, "How to Make Choosing Easier," TED talk, November 2011, http://www.ted.com/talks/sheena_iyengar_choosing_what_to_choose.

5. Stephen Ko, "Bisociation and Opportunity," in *Opportunity Identification and Entrepreneurial Behavior*, ed. John E. Butler (Greenwich, CT: Information Age Publishing, 2004), 102.

6. Dr. Seuss, *Oh, the Places You'll Go!* (New York: Random House, 1990), 6, 15, 20.

7. "Young adults want to make their own hours, come to work in their jeans and flip-flops, and save the world while they're at it." Barna, "Millennials: Big Career Goals, Limited Job Prospects," June 10, 2014, https://www.barna.org/barna-update/millennials/671-millennials-big-career-goals-limited-job-prospects.

8. Andy Chan, "Called to the Future," manuscript accepted for publication in *Theology, News & Notes* (Pasadena, CA: Fuller Theological Seminary, 2014).

CHAPTER 2: OPEN-DOOR PEOPLE AND CLOSED-DOOR PEOPLE

1. Carol Dweck, *Mindset: The New Psychology of Success* (New York: Ballantine, 2008), 3.

2. Frederick Buechner, *The Sacred Journey* (New York: HarperCollins, 1982), 104.

3. F. D. Bruner, *Matthew: A Commentary: The Churchbook: Matthew 13–28* (Grand Rapids, MI: Eerdmans, 1990), 805–6.

4. Jessica Bennett, "They Feel 'Blessed,'" *New York Times*, May 2, 2014, http://www.nytimes.com/2014/05/04/fashion/blessed-becomes-popular-word-hashtag-social-media.html.

5. Dr. Seuss, *One Fish, Two Fish, Red Fish, Blue Fish* (New York: Random House, 1960), 1, 13.

6. Dr. Seuss, *Oh, the Places You'll Go!* (New York: Random House, 1990), 5.

7. James Dunn, *Word Biblical Commentary: Romans 1–8*, vol. 38A (Waco, TX: Word, 1988).

8. Ernest Kurtz, "Spirituality and Recovery: The Historical Journey," in Ernest Kurtz, *The Collected Ernie Kurtz*, Hindsfoot Foundation Series on Treatment and Recovery (New York: Authors Choice, 2008), http://hindsfoot.org/tcek09.pdf.

9. See Dr. Seuss, *Oh, the Places You'll Go!*, 46–48.

CHAPTER 3: NO MO FOMO: OVERCOMING THE FEAR OF MISSING OUT

1. Geoffrey Mohan, "Facebook Is a Bummer, Study Says," *Los Angeles Times*, August 14, 2013, http://articles.latimes.com/2013/aug/14/science/la-sci-sn -facebook-bummer-20130814.

2. Steven Furtick, quoted in Brett and Kate McKay, "Fighting FOMO: 4 Questions That Will Crush the Fear of Missing Out," The Art of Manliness, October 21, 2013, http://www.artofmanliness.com/2013/10/21/fighting-fomo.

3. Frederick Buechner, *The Sacred Journey* (New York: HarperCollins, 1982), 107.

4. Chris Lowney, *Heroic Leadership* (Chicago: Loyola Press, 2003), 121, 29.

5. Sam Whiting, "Muni Driver Will Make New Friends, Keep the Old," *San Francisco Chronicle*, September 8, 2013, http://www.sfchronicle.com /bayarea/article/Muni-driver-will-make-new-friends-keep-the-old -4797537.php#/0.

CHAPTER 4: COMMON MYTHS ABOUT DOORS

1. John Blake, "Actually, That's Not in the Bible," *CNN Belief Blog*, June 5, 2011, http://religion.blogs.cnn.com/2011/06/05/thats-not-in-the-bible.

2. Gerald Hawthorne, *Colossians* (self-published commentary, 2010), appendix.

3. David Garrow, *Bearing the Cross* (New York: Random House, 1988), 57–58.

4. The story of the Rechabites is told in Jeremiah 35:1-19.

5. Chip Heath and Dan Heath, *Decisive* (New York: Random House, 2013), 40–41.

6. M. Craig Barnes attributes this idea to C. S. Lewis. See M. Craig Barnes, "One Calling of Many," *The Christian Century*, March 19, 2014, http://www.christiancentury.org/article/2014-03/one-calling-many.

7. Frederick Buechner, *Telling Secrets* (San Francisco: HarperSanFrancisco, 1991), HarperCollins e-book edition.

CHAPTER 5: DOOR #1 OR DOOR #2?

1. Quoted in Dallas Willard, *Hearing God* (Downers Grove, IL: InterVarsity Press, 2012), 180.

2. Archibald MacLeish, quoted in Sheena Iyengar, *The Art of Choosing* (New York: Hachette, 2010), xvii.

3. Dr. Seuss, *Oh, the Places You'll Go!* (New York: Random House, 1990), 25.

4. Barry Schwartz, "The Paradox of Choice," TED talk, July 2005, http://www.ted.com/talks/barry_schwartz_on_the_paradox_of_choice.

5. Ichak Adizes, *Managing Corporate Lifecycles* (Santa Barbara, CA: Adizes Institute Publishing, 2004), 6.

6. Chip Heath and Dan Heath, *Decisive* (New York: Random House, 2013), 10.

CHAPTER 6: HOW TO CROSS A THRESHOLD

1. Doris Kearns Goodwin, *The Bully Pulpit* (New York: Simon & Schuster, 2013), 44.

2. John Chrysostom, "Homily XXXIII" (on Hebrews 12:28-29).

3. Andy Chan, "Called to the Future," manuscript accepted for publication in *Theology, News & Notes* (Pasadena, CA: Fuller Theological Seminary, 2014).

4. Ibid.

5. Ryan Grenoble, "San Pedro Post Office Volunteers Have Been Giving Back to Community Since 1966," *Huffington Post*, August 16, 2012, http://www.huffingtonpost.com/2012/08/16/san-pedro-volunteer-post-office-_n_1790883.html.

6. "Century Marks," *Christian Century*, April 16, 2014, 9.

CHAPTER 7: WHAT OPEN DOORS WILL TEACH YOU—ABOUT YOU

1. Fyodor Dostoyevsky, *Notes from Underground*, trans. Constance Garnett, part 1, chapter 11.

2. Marcus Buckingham, *The Truth about You* (Nashville: Thomas Nelson, 2008), 41.

3. F. D. Bruner, *Matthew: A Commentary: The Churchbook: Matthew 13–28* (Grand Rapids, MI: Eerdmans, 1990), 332.

4. Warren Sazama, S.J., "Some Ignatian Principles for Making Prayerful Decisions," http://www.marquette.edu/faith/ignatian-principles-for-making-decisions.php.

CHAPTER 8: THE JONAH COMPLEX

1. A. H. Maslow, *The Farther Reaches of Human Nature* (New York: Viking, 1971), 36.

2. Ibid., 36–37.

3. Phillip Cary, *Jonah*, Brazos Theological Commentary on the Bible (Grand Rapids, MI: Brazos Press, 2008).

4. Gregg Levoy, *Callings* (New York: Harmony Books, 1997), 190.

5. Quoted in Levoy, *Callings*, 191.

6. William H. Myers, *God's Yes Was Louder than My No: Rethinking the African American Call to Ministry* (Trenton, NJ: Africa World Press, 1994), quoted in Levoy, *Callings*, 199–200.

7. Phillip Cary's commentary on Jonah points out the significance of the pairing of "great" and "evil" here in Jonah 4:1. See Cary, *Jonah*.

CHAPTER 9: THANK GOD FOR CLOSED DOORS

1. William Shakespeare, *Hamlet*, Act 5, Scene 2.

2. Frederick Buechner, *The Sacred Journey* (New York: HarperCollins, 1982), 108.

3. Dr. Seuss, *How the Grinch Stole Christmas!* (New York: Random House, 1957).

4. Jennifer Kennedy Dean, "Think Small When You Dream Big," Praying Life Foundation, April 13, 2011, http://www.prayinglife.org/2011/04 /think-small-when-you-dream-big/.

5. Portions of this section are adapted from my book *Soul Keeping: Caring for the Most Important Part of You* (Grand Rapids, MI: Zondervan, 2014), 112–15.

6. Quoted from Rudolf Bultmann in F. D. Bruner, *Matthew: A Commentary: The Churchbook: Matthew 13–28* (Grand Rapids, MI: Eerdmans, 1990), 780.

CHAPTER 10: THE DOOR IN THE WALL

1. Cornelius Plantinga Jr., *Reading for Preaching* (Grand Rapids, MI: Eerdmans, 2013), 62–63.

2. Rabbi Stephen Pearce, "Mezuzot Remind Us That Doors Hold a Symbolic Meaning," Jweekly.com, August 5, 2004, http://www.jweekly.com/article /full/23315/mezuzot-remind-us-that-doors-hold-a-symbolic-meaning/.

3. Bob Goff, *Love Does* (Nashville: Thomas Nelson, 2012), 44–45.

AFTERWORD

1. Gerald Hawthorne, *Colossians* (self-published commentary, 2010), appendix.

2. The poems in this chapter are found in Dr. Jerry Hawthorne's very moving devotional. I'm deeply indebted to him for his inspirational insights about the nature of the passage in Revelation 3 and for his thoughts that are particularly important to this final chapter.

About the Author

John Ortberg is an author, speaker, and the senior pastor of Menlo Park Presbyterian Church (MPPC) in the San Francisco Bay area. His books include *Soul Keeping*, *Who Is This Man?*, *The Life You've Always Wanted*, *Faith and Doubt*, and *If You Want to Walk on Water, You've Got to Get out of the Boat*. John teaches around the world at conferences and churches.

Born and raised in Rockford, Illinois, John graduated from Wheaton College and holds a Master of Divinity and doctorate degree in clinical psychology from Fuller Seminary. Prior to joining MPPC, John served as teaching pastor at Chicago's Willow Creek Community Church. John is a member of the Board of Trustees at Fuller Seminary, serves on the board for the Dallas Willard Center for Spiritual Formation, and is a former board member of Christianity Today International.

Now that their children are grown, John and his wife, Nancy, enjoy surfing the Pacific to help care for their souls. He can be followed on Twitter @johnortberg.

Compassion International is partnering with Tyndale House Publishers in the publication of this book.

Visit **Compassion.com/johnortberg** to see Compassion president Santiago "Jimmy" Mellado and John Ortberg discuss how readers can walk through open doors to help those in need.

If you'd like to know more about Compassion's ministry to release children from poverty in Jesus' name, visit Compassion.com.